Queen Elizabeth and the Revolt of the Netherlands

Queen Elizabeth and the Revolt of the Netherlands

CHARLES WILSON
F.B.A., Hon.Litt.D. (Groningen)
Professor of Modern History, University of Cambridge

MACMILLAN

First published 1970 by
MACMILLAN AND CO LTD
London and Basingstoke
Associated companies in New York Toronto
Dublin Melbourne Johannesburg and Madras

SBN (boards) 333 06037 7

Printed in Great Britain by
R. & R. CLARK LTD
Edinburgh

Contents

List of Plates

between pages 64 and 65

ACKNOWLEDGEMENT

The publishers wish to thank the Director, Bibliothèque Royale de Belgique, for permission to reproduce Plate I.

Preface

M Y first thanks must go to the Electors to Ford's Lectureship in English History in the University of Oxford, who honoured me with the invitation to discharge that formidable responsibility in 1969, generously interpreting the statute so as to allow me to deal with a subject which contained nearly as much Netherlands as it did English history. To Hugh Trevor-Roper, Regius Professor of Modern History in the University of Oxford, and his fellow-Electors, I am grateful for much encouragement, guidance and hospitality.

The colleagues and pupils upon whom I have from time to time inflicted discussion of problems arising from my subject are far too numerous to be thanked individually. Two must nevertheless be singled out. Vivian Fisher of Jesus College, Cambridge, very kindly read the completed manuscript, and I have benefited by a number of characteristically penetrating comments and suggestions which he made. Geoffrey Parker, Fellow of Christ's College, generously allowed me to make use of his unique knowledge of the Spanish, French and Italian archives to check and supplement my own information. I am deeply grateful to both.

Finally, it will be evident that quite apart from my own researches these lectures owe a heavy debt to many scholars, Dutch, Belgian, American and British especially, who have worked in this or related fields of inquiry. I am not less indebted to those from whose interpretations I have ventured to differ than to those with whom I have found myself in agreement.

C. W.

Prelude

THE lectures which, with necessary alterations and additions, form the basis of this book touch on many facets of English and Netherlands history. Since they are published in English, a brief note on the origins of the Netherlands question in the sixteenth century may not be out of place.[1]

The Treaty of Cateau-Cambrésis (April 1559) ended the long struggle between Valois and Habsburg which had begun with Charles VIII's mad expedition into Italy sixty-five years before. The whole configuration of European politics and diplomacy thereupon underwent a rapid and radical change. The great empire of Charles V had already been divided at his abdication three years earlier. As Holy Roman Emperor he was succeeded by his brother Ferdinand; as King of Spain, Naples and Sicily, Duke of Milan, Master of Franche-Comté, ruler of north Africa, the Philippines and large areas of America he was succeeded by his son, Philip II.

To Philip (who spoke no word of French or Flemish) also fell the overlordship of the Burgundian Netherlands. Here, since the fourteenth century, the French family of the Dukes of Burgundy had steadily won a commanding position – first acquiring Flanders, then Brabant. By 1430 they had also added Holland, Zeeland and Hainault. Luxembourg and other Walloon (French-speaking) provinces rounded off their possessions. Originally supported by the French monarchy, the Burgundians did not long conceal their ambitions to found an independent state on the flank of France. With the death of the last Duke, Charles, in 1477, Burgundy itself was isolated from its Netherlands acquisitions. Charles's daughter having married Maximilian of Habsburg, the Netherlands, now centred once again on Flanders and Brabant, became part of the Habsburg empire. Foreigners all, Burgundians and Habsburgs alike unwittingly did a great deal to create some consciousness of unity amongst the patchwork of duchies, counties and signories which made up their Netherlands possessions. They raised up a high nobility, mainly of Walloon origin, placed them in high offices of state and enriched them by grants of estates and generous endowments from taxation; they created a most exclusive club for them in the shape of the Order of the Golden Fleece; they encouraged the provincial States to send delegates to a States-General; they fashioned a common system of taxation and established their 'Stadholders' in the different provinces, selected from the highest noble families.

In spite of these innovations the centralising principle remained weak in the Low Countries. Their wealthy cities, uniquely large and numerous and peopled by an obstinately independent race of traders and craftsmen, did not take kindly to the new monarchical idea; neither did many of the large and powerful class of nobility. They too were touchily sensitive to any interference with the rights and privileges of their high status. When Philip II came to rule the Netherlands he did not come as a King. Out of his supposed seventeen 'lordships', Brabant, Gelderland, Luxembourg and Limburg recognised him as a Duke; Flanders, Holland, Zeeland, Hainault, Namur, Artois and Zutfen as a Count; elsewhere he went by even less exalted titles.[2] These states had only a rudimentary constitution in common and they spoke several different languages – Dutch, Frisian, Low German and French. Burgundian and Habsburg force had weakened but not destroyed local particularism. Interprovincial feuds continued – Gelderland against Holland and Brabant, Holland against Utrecht, Groningen against Friesland. Ghent – always a centre of radicalism and still one of the richest textile cities of Europe, though pressed increasingly hard by domestic and foreign competitors – rose in revolt against Charles V in 1539–40. The occasion was the proposal for a heavy subsidy from which Ghent boldly claimed immunity. Charles, though himself born and baptised in Ghent, showed no mercy on his fellow citizens and subjects. The ringleaders were hanged; the local magistrates were publicly and systematically humiliated and a heavy fine was levied on the whole city.

It was, then, no tame or tranquil society which Philip inherited from his predecessors. On the contrary, from the high-spirited, high-living nobility at its top to the often militant weavers, carpenters, fishermen and dock workers at its bottom, this was a turbulent and diversified society, enjoying a unique and highly individual culture of its own.

As the Low Countries passed from Charles V into the hands of Philip II, a number of external changes increased the frictions which would almost certainly have been created anyway by the

new ruler's ignorance of Netherlands affairs and the cold dislike
he showed for his new subjects. The long struggle with France had
left Spain as well as France economically exhausted. It was not
only royal treasuries but the bellies of the poor that were empty in
the 1550s and 1560s. International trade and domestic industry
were alike disrupted. Technological and market change combined
with unprecedented inflation and radical religious upheaval to
turn society into a state of flux. The formal international peace
established at Cateau-Cambrésis did not tame the forces of
violence; it only diverted them into other channels. In France,
England and the Spanish Netherlands, to say nothing of the
German states, the struggle now became local, and 'horizontal'
(between reformers and counter-reformers) as well as 'vertical'
(between class and class).

Philip's own 'reforms' applied a fresh irritant to an already
inflamed political, economic and social situation. He himself had
left the Netherlands in a rage in 1559; but not before he had heard
the nobility in 1556 censure Spain's war with the French and
denounce Spain for pursuing designs of her own in Italy that were
none of the Netherlands' business. In the year before he departed,
the States had insisted on their right to raise a subsidy only
through commissioners appointed by and accountable to themselves. Just before he finally went, the States-General in session
at Ghent had stipulated that three thousand Spanish troops
stationed in the Low Countries should go home.

When Philip departed for Spain he left affairs in the hands of a
Council of State. Dominating it was Granvelle, Bishop of Arras.
Granvelle's first act was to introduce a total reorganisation of the
Netherlands bishoprics so as to increase the capacity of the Church
to stem the rising tide of heresy; in other words to enforce ruth-
lessly the Roman Catholic religion and persecute without mercy
anything definable as a deviation from strict orthodoxy. Like
most of Philip's innovations, the reforms were not new but their
application aroused the combined opposition of nobility, clergy
and towns, much of it self-interested but some deriving from
genuine hatred of increased persecution. Persecution in itself was
not new – Charles V had introduced the Inquisition in 1522 – but
the new hard line provoked the people at large to a pitch of
excitement never reached in earlier disturbances.

Opposition to the Spanish policy of persecution began, in

medieval fashion, with the high nobility led by the Prince of Orange and the Counts of Egmont and Hoorne. It was their detestation for a man they regarded as an upstart bureaucrat which caused even Philip, remote as he now was from Netherlands affairs, to recall Granvelle to Spain. By 1565 the unrest had spread to the lesser nobility. Some five hundred of these were recruited into a league to oppose the Inquisition and the Edicts ordering the persecution of heretics. In April 1566 they marched in solemn procession to the palace of Philip's Governess, Margaret of Parma, in Brussels. When Berlaymont, a leading Walloon noble but a loyalist, contemptuously dubbed them *les gueux* ('beggars') they seized on the epithet with gusto and turned it into a title of honour.

So far the movement had embraced Catholics as well as Protestants; its impetus came if anything rather from the still politically and economically preponderant south than from the north. But the year 1566 saw a wave of Calvinist iconoclasm sweep the whole of the Netherlands from the Walloon south up as far as Friesland and Groningen in the north. Calvinism and other forms of Protestantism might as yet represent the beliefs of only a small proportion of the people but they gave the opposition a much more militant, even frenzied, character than it had revealed so far. Churches everywhere were stripped bare of ornaments. The textile districts of west Flanders and ports like Antwerp and Amsterdam, where something like a proletariat more characteristic of a later age already existed, were especially vulnerable. In the prevailing malaise that had struck down manufacturing industry, thousands of unemployed had been turned adrift, hungry and desperate. These economic factors added to the popular discontent. The first general open fighting began in 1566. It did not last long. The swift annihilation of the rebel bands by the armies of the Governess, led by loyal Walloon nobles, temporarily put an end to opposition. The Prince of Orange was forced to leave the Netherlands and take refuge on his German estates.

Nevertheless it seemed plain to Philip that the situation was too dangerous for him to rely on the doubtful loyalty of the Netherlands nobles. Next summer, in 1567, four regiments of infantry, with 1200 cavalry, set out from Italy to cross the Alps to Brussels. They arrived in August, and they were the first of many thousands who were to follow this or similar routes northwards over the next half-century. Their commander, who was to terrorise the Netherlands for the next six years, was the Duke of Alba. The phase of murderous brutality inaugurated by the new commander did not suppress the revolt; on the contrary it solidified opposition, in south and north, united Catholics and Protestants – only temporarily as it was to prove – and gave a new importance to the northern provinces. For it was here that a series of commando landings and local revolutions by the 'Sea Beggars' threw the ports of the Scheldt–Maas delta from Den Briel to Flushing on to the rebel side. Thus was created a new fortress accessible to the sea, supplied by approaches effectively controlled by the rebels. Increasingly the forces of resistance were to be concentrated here, though the unity of the rebellion as a movement of the entire Netherlands was not to be broken for another seven – it might be argued thirteen – years.

It is not my purpose here to follow the course of the Revolt as its character and objectives changed and developed; only to remark that the rebels' concept of political organisation remained consistent – as Sir George Clark has put it, 'a system of rights and privileges mutually guaranteed'. This was the idea they kept alive against all the efforts of despotism, dynasticism and arbitrary rule to suppress them. Their victory was unique in the sixteenth century. It not only produced a 'state' totally different in character from the centralised, absolutist monarchies rising to power in most other countries. It also helped to preserve and encourage ideas of constitutionalism and the rule of law in other countries. Amongst these was England, and it is with England's – and specifically Queen Elizabeth's – relations with the Netherlands that these lectures are concerned.

The Anglo-Netherlands relationship was complex, confused and stormy. The alliance with Burgundy had long been a traditional anchor of English policy, widely believed to be essential to England's security against the ancient menace from France. Spain and Spain's friends in England constantly appealed to it. But so did those who now believed that Spain was a traitor to the ideas and ideals of the Burgundian alliance. Who, then, after 1564–7, could rightly claim to be true heir to the Burgundian traditions? Who was now England's proper ally? Was it Philip? Or his rebellious subjects? Even more difficult, who was entitled to be the Burgundian torch-bearer after 1579–85 when the southern provinces crept back to Spanish obedience and the revolt continued only in the seven northern provinces? Where did the strategic and economic advantage of England now lie? To these and many other questions, different voices returned different answers. For alongside the physical conflict and the economic warfare, another battle was also in progress: the battle of ideas. Those on one side believed that rebellion of any kind constituted a general threat to authority and therefore to the very stability of the social order. Those on the other believed that the victims of tyranny deserved help, whoever they were. It is with the gradual unwinding of such problems and the involuntary, reluctant formulation of their solutions that the following pages deal.

The Netherlands: boundaries and divisions

1 English Intervention and the Pattern of Revolt

ON 23 February 1587 the House of Commons listened to a rousing speech by the Member for Warwick. Job Throckmorton was a learned Puritan zealot, commanding a rich flow of invective with which he drenched all those whom he supposed to be the mortal enemies of England, its Queen and the true religion. Successively and with relish, he excoriated the 'filthiness of life' of Catherine de Medici and her offspring; 'the beast of Rome with a mark on his forehead'; Philip of Spain, licentious and incestuous; the Scottish Dame ('by the good Providence of God brought low to the dust') and her son 'the young imp of Scotland', to name only a few. England was surrounded by the powers of darkness. 'Whither then,' he cried, 'shall we direct our course? The very finger of God directs us to the Low Countries, as though to say: "There only is the means of your safety, there only is the passage laid open to you, there only, and nowhere else, is the vent of your commodities." ' And much more.[1]

An innocent listener might have been forgiven for supposing that the Member for Warwick's patriotic sentiments would evoke a sympathetic 'amen' from those responsible for England's foreign policy. Was not France the ancient enemy? Had not the Queen been excommunicated by Pius V? Had not Gregory XIII planned her assassination? Had she not very justifiably expelled two Spanish ambassadors in succession for plotting against her life? Were not her troops even at that moment fighting in the Low Countries to preserve what was left of them from the King of Spain? And was she not bound by solemn treaty to support her allies the Dutch until they should have extracted a secure peace from their Spanish oppressors? Yes, indeed, all this was true. But it did not prevent the Queen, nervous and irascible over the execution of Mary, Queen of Scots and the total confusion of Leicester's strategy in the Netherlands, from clapping Throckmorton into jail for several months to reflect on the mysterious ways of Providence and the hardly less inscrutable purposes of Gloriana.

Throckmorton's fate will serve as a suitable introduction to the historiography of a subject of oriental deviousness. At its centre is the Queen herself, part woman, part man, part English, part Welsh, as dazzlingly seductive to some historians as she is repellent to others. When the female element is dominant, passionate and ungovernable: when the male element takes control, capable of the courage of a Churchill, the oratorical fire of a Lloyd George or the indolence and indecision of a Baldwin. Our historiography is strewn with her victims and her critics. It is bedevilled by legends deeply rooted in patriotism, antique xenophobia and musty theology. It is both lit and obscured by the pious labours of historians who have from time to time backed Britain, dreamed of a Great Netherlands or attempted the Sisyphean rescue of Philip II's reputation. Our Tudor specialists have liberally decorated their part of the historical preserve with warnings to intending poachers. More merciful than some of his colleagues, Professor Williams has left the gate ajar: 'facts,' he has written of the Elizabethan puzzle, 'may present themselves in a new pattern when seen by fresh eyes.'[2]

The interpretation of the Queen's handling of the Netherlands episode which follows is not so much a novel view as a reversion to an older view. If it conflicts with current opinion, it is because I do not feel able to subscribe to a view – as I see it, a parochial and uncritical view – of Queen Elizabeth and Burghley as the natural and almost infallible executors of the English 'national interest'; of Walsingham and his companion Marian exiles, together with William the Silent and Oldenbarneveldt, as evident spokesmen for sectarian bias or alien vested interests. I believe that important contemporary research into foreign, especially Netherlands and Spanish, sources should make us reflect again on English policy towards Spain and the Netherlands in Elizabeth's reign.[3]

I need not waste time in justifying the historical importance of the Revolt itself. Its exploration by mid-nineteenth-century scholars – Gachard, Fruin, Groen van Prinsterer, Bakhuizen van den Brink and of course John Lothrop Motley – forms one of the most remarkable chapters in the pioneering of scientific history. Motley's classic description of it is today out of favour, but his judgement still holds good: here was 'one of the leading events of modern times. Without the birth of this great Commonwealth the various historical phenomena of the sixteenth and following centuries must either not have existed or have presented themselves under essential modifications.' Almost every historian who has studied the Revolt since has endorsed that verdict. Of the origins and course of the Revolt, or the Eighty Years War, as the Dutch themselves call it, it need only be said now that it was essentially a European and not a local affair. It drew in and enveloped not only the old Burgundian territories in the Netherlands and Spain but France and England as well, to say nothing of a variety of German princes large and small. Enormous mercenary armies tramped northwards over the Alps and westwards from Germany. Spaniards and Italians left the sun and wine of Italy to fight and mutiny, fester and die in the cold, foggy swamps of Holland and Zeeland. Here they came face to face with equally miserable bands of Irish, Scots and English, usually ragged, often half-naked, invariably unpaid, ill-led and discontented. Many on both sides knew and cared nothing about the causes or objects of the war in which they were entangled, and from time to time diverted on to their own officers, or the local peasantry and burghers, the savagery which they were in theory paid to inflict on the enemy. This was an international war, a civil war, a religious war, a class war all rolled into one and it spanned eight of the most savage decades in the history of modern warfare.

It is not my intention in these lectures to deal with the course of the Revolt in more detail than is necessary to clarify my theme and attempt to justify my opinions regarding English policy towards the Revolt. It began as 'a revolt of mediaevalism', if you like, of indignant feudal magnates against a clumsy and brutal attempt by Philip II to create a centralised state, based on Brussels, out of the easy-going, relatively liberal confusion of principalities he had inherited from his predecessors. It then turned through bewildering vicissitudes of success and failure into a more recognisably modern struggle against a foreign occupation, against the Inquisition, against dynasticism and bureaucracy in all their political and economic manifestations. The nineteenth-century scholars who investigated the Revolt were not entirely wrong in sniffing an air of liberty (in the later sense) in sixteenth- and seventeenth-century Holland. But in large measure what was at stake was less 'liberty' than 'liberties' – privileges – feudal, oligarchic, economic, religious, to which different groups considered themselves entitled as by custom or right.

In an unusually crisp rebuke to the Spanish envoy in London, Burghley once observed: 'You people are of such a sort that wherever you set foot no grass grows.' That was what the Revolt was about. Its end was a divided Netherlands: in the northern half of the old Burgundian Netherlands an oligarchic, federal republic of merchants; in the southern half, so prominent in the revolt of the early years, the so-called 'obedient provinces' reduced once more to Spanish control. To attempt to identify a single cause, a single man or a single class of men as the sole spring of resistance is to waste time. In the words of a Dutch historian who analysed the historiography of the Revolt ten years ago, the Revolt was not a bloc movement: there was 'a number of revolts representing the interests and the ideals of various social, economic and ideological groups: revolts which sometimes run parallel, sometimes conflict with one another, and at other times coalesce into a single movement'.[4]

A bird's-eye view of events seems at first sight to confirm the magnitude of the Queen's achievement in relation to the Revolt. England survived and in a measure prospered. So did the Dutch Republic. Spain, though still wealthy and powerful, was humbled and weakened, even if not permanently defeated. France emerged from the chaotic divisions of nearly half a century. Swift, bold decisions, like the seizure of Alba's treasure at Plymouth, are seen to punctuate the endless ponderings of Burghley and the prevarications of the Queen. The broken pledges, the subterfuges and the brinkmanship are admitted, but they are woven into the pattern of masterful, purposeful diplomacy, on which is stamped its own proof: all's well that ends well. The Stuarts can take the blame for what happened later.

In the Netherlands specifically, Professor Wernham has argued persuasively in favour of Queen Elizabeth's policy towards the Dutch. Guided not by any liking for rebels or Calvinism, but by considerations of England's defence and security, she set herself to get the Spanish army out of the Netherlands without letting in England's traditional enemy, the French. The Netherlands would remain under nominal Spanish suzerainty. There could be no question of their independence. They must be content with their ancient liberties. This policy, it is argued, made sense until 1585 when it was finally abandoned. In the 1570s it is held to have very nearly succeeded during the brief period of national union of loyalists and rebels that followed the revulsion against the Spanish Fury of 1576, when bands of mutineers ravaged Antwerp and other cities. Like Sir John Neale, Professor Wernham blames the Earl of Leicester in person for the disasters of the English expeditionary force from 1585 to 1587.[5] But Elizabeth's policy is seen to be fundamentally right. Her weakness lay, the argument continues, in 'her inability to control its instruments'.[6]

The Armada episode, with its hairsbreadth escape from disaster for England, is less easy to fit into this pattern. Nevertheless, escape England did and that is enough. The Queen is defended for trying, as late as 1598, to persuade the Dutch to accept Spanish sovereignty of a nominal (if absurd) kind. This tail-end of the argument is held to justify all the more clearly the underlying basis of the Queen's policy. For if, a century later, the Netherlands were to be so weak and vulnerable to the threat from Louis XIV, does not this justify Elizabeth's refusal to promote their independence?

Dr Rowse has rebuffed with chivalrous indignation those who criticise the Queen's policy in the Netherlands. His argument that the critics have been naïvely ignorant of the problems she faced is important. I shall explain why it does not satisfy my own thoughts. Professor Elton admits that Elizabeth was often dilatory and hesitant but ultimately he too has no fundamental criticism of her policy. Mr Beckingsale writes persuasively of the combination of luck and judgement with which the Queen and Burghley pursued their English common-sense solutions while an outside world tore itself to pieces on rival ideologies and ambitions.[7]

Such are some of the arguments marshalled to defend the Queen against critics ancient and modern. They will be examined in subsequent lectures, not with any presumption that better answers to the Queen's dilemmas could have been easily provided. Her skill and courage survived her enemies; so did her luck. Retrospective omniscience and a Whiggish acceptance that whatever was was right are the twin rocks between which the historian must steer. It will be assumed in these lectures that the Queen's prime duty was owed to her own state and nation, not to any other, however gallant or deserving. Equally, the evidence used to support or criticise her policy must be the contemporary evidence of men who had some serious claim to represent informed opinion, not merely the retrospective wisdom of historians conveniently placed to add to or subtract from their case facts unknown at the time. The question to be asked is this. Are we watching in these years the pursuit of rational ends by consistent statesmanlike diplomacy? Or are we rationalising into policies, *ex post facto*, what was, in reality, a succession of shifts and muddles into which the Queen stumbled because she was obsessed by understandable but irrational fears – the fear of rebellions, the fear of France especially – or the obverse of those fears – the deference towards Philip, the desire to recover Calais?

In 1931 the late Pieter Geyl published his study of the Revolt.[8] It was designed to destroy the traditional Calvinist and liberal patterns of explanation of the birth of the Dutch Republic. The doyen of the Calvinist historians, Groen van Prinsterer, had seen the Revolt as a religious, a Calvinist phenomenon. Others had taken a more libertarian view. For Bakhuizen van den Brink, it was the embodiment of the spirit of civil liberty. Motley, writing in the Anglo-American high liberal tradition, followed Bakhuizen rather than Groen. For this undenominational Bostonian human-ist,[9] the intolerance, brutality and iconoclasm of the Calvinists was hardly less repellent than the faggots and thumbscrews of the Inquisition. But for Groen, the vague latitudinarianism of Motley was scarcely less dangerous than the Scarlet Woman in person. Unitarians (and Motley was nominally a Unitarian) were hardly Christians. They were mere Deists. They tolerated a chapel service where, wrote Groen, 'they read verses from Dryden or other English poets on the existence of God and the immortality of the soul. They deliver a discourse on some point of morality, and all is said.'[10]

Whether they favoured a civil or religious interpretation, the nineteenth-century historians agreed to endow the rebellious Protestant north (as they believed it to be) with a special virtue. A latent propensity to freedom or truth might be derived either from spiritual revelation or from those Teutonic origins which rendered them (to Motley for example) morally and physically superior to their Latin or Celtic opponents. Here was the simple explanation of their success. They were tougher, they were more virtuous and they were right. A manifest Dutch destiny underpinned the enterprises of William the Silent, Maurice of Nassau and Oldenbarneveldt. By contrast the Belgians, contam-inated by Spanish decadence and Popery, to say nothing of Latin and Gallic racial weaknesses, were predictably crushed under the heel of Spain.

The fallacies in such arguments became more obvious as systematic research threw into relief some basic truths about the Revolt. First, many northern areas were strongly Catholic; many areas in the south equally strongly Protestant. Second, in the early stages of revolt resistance was as much Catholic as Protestant. Third, it was only because of the course of events that a gradual polarisation of the forces of resistance took place in the north. The work of Muller, Asher and others revealed the full debt of the northern Republic to the old south.[11] 'Here is Antwerp become Amsterdam,' cried an immigrant of the nineties from the south. War, religion, persecution, economic insecurity steadily drove north across land, and west across the water, some of the most vigorous men and women of Ghent, Bruges, Ypres, Antwerp and their satellite towns and villages. The south was the womb of the Republic. Migrants from the south played a major part in creating the northern economy – the new silk industry of Amsterdam, the linen industry of Haarlem, the great cloth industry of Leyden, the banking and trading houses, the great colonial companies; and they were often (but not always) convinced and obstinate Protestants. Their brothers and sisters, uncles, aunts and cousins were to be found in the London suburbs, Norwich, Colchester, Rye, Canterbury and Sandwich, spreading the same theologies and the same industrial techniques. This was the Protestant diaspora. It influenced profoundly not only the economy but the culture and politics of the north.[12]

Neither Motley nor even Geyl fully grasped the significance of these movements. Geyl's central text was provided by a friend and follower of William the Silent, Geldorp. The best centre of resistance to the Spaniard, wrote Geldorp in 1570, was not the ancient political axis of Brussels but the north, with its rivers and islands. Here was the great redoubt, north and west of the great rivers which traversed the Low Countries from east to west. This was the germ of the idea brilliantly translated by Geyl into a historical interpretation which revolutionised twentieth-century thinking about the strategy of the Netherlands Revolt. But Geyl's main interest was political: before his eyes was the vision of a Great Netherlands state.

Geyl's theory was this: the split into a predominantly Protestant north and a Catholic south was not predetermined by any divergences of *character* between the peoples affected, as previous students of the Revolt had suggested. It was only the military force deployed by a foreign ruler in a very specific geographical and topographical setting which redistributed forces and estranged the two regions. 'The outcome was determined by the great rivers.' Brabant, Flanders and the Walloon provinces lay open to the enemy and were therefore detached. In this way, earlier interpretations of the split which assumed some inherent divergence of character between north and south were brusquely dispatched. For Geyl, earlier historians were for the most part victims of ignorance or prejudice. Motley was a 'New England Presbyterian', ignorant of many basic features of Netherlands history; Groen van Prinsterer was the embodiment of the Calvinist historical myth. Robert Fruin, sometimes regarded as the Dutch Ranke, alone deserved serious consideration.[13]

Geyl was not content to state his case and leave it. Scattered throughout his works are repeated asseverations of his river defence theory.[14] Passionately attached to the cause of a 'Great Netherlands', he was one of the academic prophets of Benelux. His entire history bore retrospective witness to the cultural unity of the Netherlands and it carries all the stamp of his passionate conviction that this unity was destroyed only by the accident of war – war waged by the King of Spain against his Netherlands dominions. I do not mean to suggest that Geyl was simply a polemicist. He felt the historian's need to *explain* great historical events. His predecessors (he thought) had failed to do this in any way convincing to a rational mind. He supplied what they had failed to deliver, and he drove home his answer repeatedly and effectively. So effectively that another distinguished Dutch historian has gone on record as saying that opinion today 'accepts' Geyl's view that the split 'was determined essentially by the course of the war in which the great rivers played the part of natural strategic frontiers'.[15]

There can be no doubt that Geyl's study has been the most potent influence in shaping current opinion on the nature and outcome of the Revolt. His contribution to this particular debate of historians has a permanent value. But it is time to look at it critically. Geyl himself never did this. He did not deepen or develop his interpretation as time went by. The polemicist in his nature preferred to pass on to new battle grounds. The rout and massacre of the tribes of Toynbee and Carr[16] was more exhilarating than the continued pursuit of the Spanish *tercios*. Yet his campaigns were still inspired by his formative years as a student of the historiography of the Revolt. These had imbued him with a deep distaste for historical determinism. His formidable polemical energies were still reserved for the offensive against those historians in whom he detected propensities towards such determinism. Yet, ironically, by his brilliant and influential analysis, this most determined of anti-determinists was – quite unintentionally – creating something like his own brand of determinism. It differed from preceding brands by being rooted in geography and topography rather than in national or religious characteristics. But many of Geyl's followers have certainly interpreted his more dogmatic statements of his theory to mean that it was topography which ensured the success of the Dutch Republic and dictated the failure of the south.

It is not my intention to try and argue Geyl's interpretation out of existence. On the contrary, it contains a basic truth which was grasped by contemporaries – indeed it was rescued by Geyl from friends of William the Silent like Geldorp whose views had been lost in the clouds of theological dust which hung over the historiography of the Revolt for over three centuries. But if applied in the most literal forms in which Geyl and others have stated it, the strategic topographical theory would leave me with very little to talk about. The capacity of Queen Elizabeth to influence the course of the Revolt would be an illusion. The role of William the Silent, Maurice or Oldenbarneveldt would be reduced to little more than that of spectators of the ineluctable victory of offence over defence south of the great rivers and of defence over offence in the battle for the Holland–Zeeland redoubt lying behind the unassailable right banks of the great rivers. But there are several reasons why I have concluded that my subject not only exists but is crucial to a fuller understanding of the destinies of both England and the Republic.

First, the length of the struggle alone should make us hesitate before accepting a simplistic view of its course and destiny. Thirteen years elapsed between the start of the Revolt and the breakaway of those southern Walloon provinces which signed the Treaty of Arras. Eighteen years passed before Antwerp fell to

Spain and before Flanders was exposed to the full force of Parma.
The Eighty Years War had run more than half its course before
Dutch and Spaniards concluded the Truce of 1609 which admitted
the *fact* of partition.

Penetrating within the northern 'redoubt', the Spaniards had
successfully laid siege to towns like Haarlem and Zierikzee. But
Amsterdam remained obstinately loyal and Catholic until 1578,
over a decade after the rebellion had broken out. The ultimate
frontiers of the Republic were not to be based on the great rivers
at all, but ran well to the south and east of them. All this suggests
that the outcome of the war was affected and determined by com-
binations of factors far more complex than those which can be
encapsulated in the Geyl 'river line' formula in its cruder forms.
The topographical theory needs to be reformulated to correspond
with some elementary facts of warfare and politics which were
neglected or misunderstood by Geyl.

Let me put it in another way: to read Geyl's account is more
often than not to have the impression of mobile warfare in which
large armies of infantry and some cavalry clashed, only in the end
to face each other across the Rhine, Waal, Lek or Maas. These are
assumed to have formed impassable barriers to the Spaniards
attempting to break in from the south or wheel round from the
east. But this is a serious misunderstanding of the military situation.
The sixteenth century was an age of siege warfare rather than of
mobile warfare. Notwithstanding a few pitched battles in open
country, the Netherlands campaigns were no exception. Within
the original seventeen provinces lay more than 200 walled cities,
150 chartered towns and more than 6000 villages. The whole area
was guarded by some sixty fortresses of massive strength. Pictorial
representations of the time illustrate vividly these massive and
costly urban fortifications; and they girdled no less formidably the
rich and powerful cities of the south like Ghent, Antwerp or
Bruges than they did the smaller and as yet less affluent towns of
the north. Many of these strongly fortified towns were built by
rivers, largely because these provided the cheapest form of transport for food and materials in peacetime; and, hopefully, an extra
defence against attack in war. But if strategy was mishandled, the
river access could become a positive menace to security, as
Antwerp was to discover in 1585.

Warfare in such a highly urbanised country was essentially a game of time, supplies, morale – and wits. Against the new arts of town fortification imported from Italy were pitted the miner and the sapper, heavier cannon and battering-rams, and the omnipresent weapons of disease and hunger. Until the real nature of warfare is more accurately anatomised it is easy to dismiss town garrison troops as mere parasites. On the contrary, the morale of a town's defenders and the skill of its commanders (or the lack of them) were the key to many strategically critical victories and defeats of the Eighty Years War. Thus politics and religion come back into the calculation. Morale was often of greater consequence than the mere presence of a river, which rarely, in the campaigning season, offered any insuperable obstruction to armies of either side. Sluys was lost to Parma in the spring of 1587 although it had access to the sea and was protected by deliberate flooding. In the following year Bergen-op-Zoom, which relied more on its fortifications, was saved from a Spanish army of 20,000 besiegers by the crafty ingenuity of Lord Willoughby and his commanders. Armies were now larger than ever – Spain certainly had 86,000 men in all in the Netherlands at the peak of her strength – but they were dispersed over large areas and a multiplicity of tasks.[17] It was not difficult to fling a bridge of boats at vulnerable points across rivers that were generally slow-moving. In winter rivers and lakes were often frozen. Troops could march over or along them, dragging cannon and equipment after them.

The hard core of fact underlying Geyl's argument was well put by an anonymous English author writing on the eve of the Second Anglo-Dutch War. His booklet, *The Dutch Drawn to the Life* (1664), was intended to inform English opinion on the characteristics of the by then potential enemy, the Dutch. It was in the form of a dialogue:

Questioner: I pray, Sir, what is their strength by land?
Answer: The sea, rivers, islands make it invincible . . . it is the great Bog of Europe, not such another Marsh in the World, a National Quagmire that they can overflow at pleasure.

This conception of a terrain well-suited to guerrilla resistance fighting differs from Geyl's 'strong, strategic barrier of rivers traversing the Netherlands from east to west . . .'[18] which held up Montgomery as well as Parma! In reality, of course, the strategic situations were not in any way comparable. Weapons, transport

and communications media and numbers were all totally transformed. Yet even without such contrasts, the facts of geography
would be inadequate to explain the success of northern resistance.
Parliament did not win the English Civil War simply because the
eastern half of England was richer than the west and north. The
Hollanders and Zeelanders did not hold out against the Spaniards
simply because they were fortunate enough to inhabit a bog.
Physical assets were vital, but without leadership and luck they
would not have been transmuted into effective resistance. The
outcome of a struggle in which topography, political leadership,
ideology and social structure were all combined was not predictable. The only observers in the early stages who thought it was,
like Elizabeth and Burghley, forecast victory for Spain, now
emerging triumphant from the Treaty of Cateau-Cambrésis and
endowed with all the rich plunder of her colonial conquests.

Everything seemed to turn on the strength of resistance and the
quality of local leadership. This, however, was not always equal
to the task of defence, including the potent attractions of Spanish
ducats. Before the anti-Spanish forces, Protestant and Catholic,
joined in the brief alliance of 1576, Zierikzee, regarded by William
the Silent as the key to the union of Holland and Zeeland, fell
to the besiegers. So did Haarlem, one of the most populous and
industrious cities of the north. Leyden only escaped by a miracle.
These were in the area *behind* the so-called river defence line.
On the other hand, Mechlin in the south, well fortified, was
surrendered by the Seigneur de Bours, a recent re-convert to the
Roman Church. The price Alexander Farnese paid him was 5000
florins and the command of an infantry regiment. The fate of
Groningen and a number of neighbouring cities of the north-east
in 1580 was to be settled by the bargain struck by Georges de
Lalaing, Count of Rennenberg, Stadholder of Friesland and
Groningen, with Farnese. And Rennenberg was the younger
brother of one of William's closest friends in the opening phases
of revolt, Count Hoogstraten.* Again, as in England sixty years
hence, the shadow of political and religious division was often
to fall across the brotherhoods and cousinhoods which composed
the traditional ruling class of the Netherlands.

The surrender of the vital town of Maastricht (1579) illustrated
clearly the nature of siege warfare. Farnese simply ground down

* Died of wounds in battle, 1568.

the defence by sheer weight of numbers and money. Antwerp finally capitulated (1585) because in the prevailing muddle its defence, not in itself an insuperable problem, was divided amongst too many leaders, none of them capable of enforcing an effective strategy.*

The problems were not all on one side. English – more probably Irish – mercenaries, starving, unclothed and unpaid, betrayed Deventer (1587). Spanish commanders had been similarly robbed by mutiny of what seemed like certain victory in Zeeland in 1575–6, and Farnese, like his predecessors, spent a large part of his military career warning Philip of the risks of leaving the Spanish army unpaid and underfed. Again, the fortunes of Spanish armies in the Netherlands were affected by contingencies other than local and domestic ones. The Netherlands struggle was not merely a local matter or even simply a civil war. It was part of a vast international and intercontinental dispute involving France and England as well as Spain. The theatre of war in the Low Countries was part of a much larger one that included northern France, parts of western Germany and the Mediterranean. At four critical points in the war the Spanish High Command was compelled to abandon the attack against the Netherlands and turn its attentions elsewhere. In 1572 Alba was distracted by the operations of William's brother Louis on the French border. In 1574 Holland was denuded of Spanish troops to meet the threat from Louis of Nassau.

In 1587–8 Farnese was ordered to mass a great army near the Flemish coast to join forces with an Armada for the invasion of England. In 1590 Henry IV was threatening Paris. Once again Parma had to divert his forces and the Dutch rebels won a final vital breathing-space.

Such contingencies opened the door to Elizabethan policy and gave it a critical role. They are mentioned in Geyl's narrative. But he passes swiftly over them to return to his river defence theory. They were difficult to fit into his grand plan.[19] Nor does he do more than mention a socio-political factor which will occupy at least one of these lectures and will be seen to condition the rest. This was the dominant position in the south Netherlands of a rich and powerful nobility largely (though not exclusively) of French-speaking Walloon origin – a great class comprising the

* See Ch. 4.

houses of Croy, Lannoy, Lalaing, Ligne, Glymes, Berlaymont and scores of others. They drew their wealth from land, property and office. They were proud, quarrelsome and not as a class over-burdened with intelligence. How different from the north! In Holland and Zeeland the merchant oligarchs were steadily con-solidating their control of urban affairs. There was a sizeable landed nobility in Gelderland and a numerous rural gentry in Friesland. But Holland – urban, commercial middle-class Holland – was ultimately to dominate the Republic through her wealth and power, supplying in the end not far short of two-thirds of the Republic's revenues.

Although many of their possessions were in the south, members of the noble class were elected to the principal offices of state throughout all the 'seventeen' Netherlands provinces. Aremberg, a member of the Ligne family of Hainault, was Stadholder of Groningen, Friesland and Overysel. So, later, was Rennenberg, who was a Lalaing. Meghen, Stadholder of Gelderland, was a Brimeu. Hoorne, Admiral of the Netherlands and Stadholder of Gelderland, was a Montmorenci. William the Silent was one of the not very numerous exceptions to the general rule of aristocratic Walloon predominance:

> Wilhelmus van Nassauwe
> Ben ick van Duitse bloet

as the Netherlands anthem still proclaims. Even William's German origins were less important than his great stretches of territory in the southern Netherlands, Brabant, Luxembourg, Flanders, Franche-Comté, to say nothing of Dauphiné, Charolais, the sovereign principality of Orange, and claims to the Kingdom of Arles as well as to numerous estates in Italy and other titles by the score. But his heart was in the very centre of the Netherlands, in Brabant, of which he owned roughly a quarter. His country seat lay at Breda; his town palace in Brussels. In 1559 he was created Stadholder of Holland, Zeeland and Utrecht by Philip II.[20]

Neither the Burgundians nor the Habsburgs had spared any effort to attach this powerful noble class firmly to the monarchy – through the formation of the Order of the Golden Fleece, through lavish grants of lands and offices. Their influence was not confined therefore to the French-speaking Walloon provinces whence so many of them came – Artois, Walloon Flanders, Hainault especially. It stretched right across the linguistic boundary which ran along a line just south of Dunkirk–Brussels–Maastricht–Luxembourg, taking in not only the Dutch-speaking provinces south of the great rivers but those far northwards up to Holland and Groningen. They were the natural political and military leaders of the Low Countries.

It was from this class of great nobility that the original initiative of the Revolt came; it was directed against Philip's attempt to impose his absolute authority on what had previously been a rich jumble of duchies, counties and seignories, to say nothing of bishoprics. But the state of mind of the whole class was ambiguous, schizophrenic. Requesens is regularly found complaining of the close co-operation between the so-called 'loyal' nobles and the rebels, long before they joined up in 1576. On the one hand, they were outraged by the invasion of their traditional rights and privileges by Philip. On the other, the pull of old loyalty to the sovereign was immensely strong; so were the material attractions of the sovereign's favours to the faithful.

The struggle to possess the bodies and souls of the nobility is the essence of the Revolt in the crucial 1570s. Yet little is made of it in Geyl's narrative. For in so far as it *is* considered important, it must argue the existence of a potential source of division between north and south *before* Philip put matters to the test of force. Yet what Geyl played down is at the heart of the Anglo-Netherlands problem of the period. It was to take Elizabeth many long years to adjust herself – if she ever did – to the idea that tradesmen could create a nation-state or that they were fit and proper persons for a monarch to deal with.* Her eye was on princes and nobles, and it was the divisions within the Netherlands nobility over the policy towards Spain which were a major cause of her fatal prevarication and hesitation.

Why were political and economic relations between England and the Netherlands so crucially important? Before the Treaty of Cateau-Cambrésis which followed swiftly upon Elizabeth's accession, diplomatic relations with the Habsburg Emperor had rested upon Henry VIII's Treaty of Windsor of 1521 with Charles V. It was honoured more in the breach than in the observance, but that did not make it unique. In its total cynicism, its mixture of long-term ideology and short-term materialism and

* See p. 40, 128.

Machtpolitik, the diplomacy of the fluid, mercurial world of the sixteenth century was more like today's mixture of intrigue and force in the never-ending tug-of-war over disputed sovereignties and boundaries in Africa, the Middle East or Central Europe than the relatively settled conventions ruling international relations between the stabilised states of the West today.

The *Magnus Intercursus* of 1496 was similarly held to govern economic relations, but it, too, provoked a stream of acrimonious controversies that sprang from the difficulties of interpreting a treaty at once vague and static in relation to a trade that was dynamic and changing.

For Charles V the principal anxiety was strategic.[21] England, as 'Lord of the Channel', held the key to communications between his Spanish and Netherlands possessions. A friendly England made it easier to wage war on France from the north. A hostile England menaced the Netherlands themselves. For England, the right government in the Low Countries was even more important. Given the sandbanks of the Netherlands coast and the prevailing south-westerly winds, it was easier for a hostile force to invade England than for an invading force to land in the Netherlands against any kind of opposition. The Armada was to make the dilemma clear. 'An alliance with England', wrote Mattingley, 'was the strongest card the Emperor could hold.'[22]

The ideal of the Burgundian alliance continued to mesmerise Elizabeth. Fitfully but powerfully, she was haunted by the spectre of what Wotton, one of her diplomatic Commissioners at Cateau-Cambrésis, called 'the aencyent immortal hatredde' of the French for England.[23] Both the English and Netherlands governments continued throughout the sixteenth century to try and call up the spirit of the old Anglo-Burgundian alliance; but in reality the accession of Philip of Spain had changed the Anglo-Netherlands relationship in a vital respect. The Netherlands were henceforth merely a pawn in the Spanish diplomatic game. If they were to fulfil this role to Philip's satisfaction he needs must suppress their local liberties; in Sir Walter Raleigh's words, 'Turklike . . . tread under his feet all their national and fundamental laws, privileges and ancient rights'. In this admittedly frightening situation, faced by the apparently overwhelming power of Spain and the ancient fear of France, Elizabeth took refuge in a bewildering succession of expedients in her Netherlands policy. I shall in due course examine their credibility and their results. For the moment, I will only call attention to a few salient features.

The 'seventeen provinces' were already the most advanced economy in the world. As the glories of north Italy faded and the Hanse lost its old momentum, the Netherlands swept all before them. By the mid-sixteenth century Antwerp, the largest city, had become the entrepôt of the western world, the market for Portuguese spices, Italian woollens and silks, south German metals, American silver and, above all, English cloth. Its population doubled in the first half of the sixteenth century to reach a figure of 100,000. London, the principal outlet and inlet for English overseas trade, was still Antwerp's satellite.[24] Urged on by the falling value of the pound sterling and currency debasement, English cloth exporters reaped a rich, if temporary, harvest. In the peak year 1550 they sold overseas over 132,000 pieces of cloth. This was nearly three times the figure of half a century earlier, and a very high proportion of the total was handled by the Merchant Adventurers Company through their staple at Antwerp. Even in the 1560s, when the boom was subsiding, this English colony of traders still accounted for somewhere between a quarter and a half of Antwerp's entire trade, inwards and outwards.

The terms of the Anglo-Netherlands marriage settlement seemed handsome. Alas! they did not ensure connubial bliss. As so often in history, what look like economic interests powerful enough to swing politics in their wake turn out in reality to be a puny thing, pathetically vulnerable to the slings and arrows of outrageous politics. Even before the revolt broke out in earnest in 1566–8, the signs became ominous that Antwerp's hegemony was in danger. Philip's accession was the sign for English merchants to start looking for alternatives. It was an old game for the Adventurers to play off Antwerp against Middelburg, Bergen-op-Zoom, Hamburg, Emden or Stade. But in 1563–4 the game turned into serious economic warfare. Even during the relatively responsible regency of Margaret of Parma it became plain that the Spanish element in the council of government for the Netherlands was entirely insouciant about the fate of Antwerp's trade. The friction between Spanish officialdom and the Antwerp city fathers was so sharp that Cardinal Granvelle went through an elaborate pretence of supporting the manufacturers of the New Draperies round Ypres against the competition of imported English cloths – those same

Calvinists of Ypres who were already setting out for Norwich or Leyden in search of freedom to exercise their religion and trade! To the attempts of the Prince of Orange, in conjunction with the Antwerp economic liberals, to negotiate the resumption of trade with England, Granvelle replied with a sneer at 'ces jeunes seigneurs' who had no understanding of English commercial or diplomatic tactics. As the rebellion simmered, the merchant community tried desperately to restore the *Magnus Intercursus*. But as Alba took up his office Gresham wrote from Antwerp that business was doomed under the tyranny of the Governor.[25] Here were the roots of that rational, commercial distrust of dynastic and state intervention in economic affairs which was to become the theme of Dutch merchant opinion down to the French Revolution.

Nor was Elizabeth's attitude to trade markedly different from that of her fellow-princes. Her own Merchant Adventurers in Antwerp received summary orders not only in regard to trade, discipline and the disposal of their funds but in matters of religion as well. The English colony was chiefly valuable to the Queen for the security it could provide as collateral for Gresham's fund-raising operations. At high cost, Antwerp was the chief centre for English government loans from 1544 to 1574.[26] In little more than a decade, Gresham alone negotiated loans totalling nearly three-quarters of a million pounds sterling, from 1553 to 1564. The proceeds went to London in gold or silver, or were spent in the Netherlands on war equipment – gunpowder, saltpetre, bow staves, harquebuses, harnesses, corslets and so on.[27]

The Habsburgs, Italian Princes and Popes, and the Vasas after them, pawned their mines of gold, silver, copper or iron. Elizabeth, whose mines were largely coal mines[28] leased out at poorish rates, pawned her merchants and their property in trade. Economic and social objectives ran a poor second to politics and diplomacy in her policies. Occasional bouts of anxiety might attack her and her ministers when unemployment threatened riots in Wiltshire, Gloucestershire or other cloth-making areas. But generally tradesmen were there to be used for the higher reasons of state. These were political and diplomatic; economic only in so far as power had to be sustained by economic means. And if this was her attitude to her own merchants, how much more so to the mercantile oligarchs who were the main prop of the Prince of Orange? For they were not merely tradesmen but rebels. They cost money.

They upset every idea in her intensely conservative mental cornucopia about the way society should be ordered and government should work. For her, the defects of the economic and social structure of the Netherlands were counter-balanced only by its traditional character of a dependency under a sovereign monarch, and by those aristocratic elements in its social order, represented by the Order of the Golden Fleece, whose duty was to uphold authority when it was threatened by fanaticism or popular rule. Until the final decade of the reign she could not bring herself to believe that the Netherlands could have or ought to have any independent future. Yet her reign saw England ever more intricately involved with the fate of the Netherlands.

Historians tracing out the attempts of Spain, France and England to bend the seventeen provinces to their respective purposes or sovereignties are apt to forget – as did the contemporary princes of Europe – that they are speaking of an area approximately three-fifths of the size of England itself. England's population may have risen rapidly in the second half of the century to reach a figure of approximately four million by 1600. The total Netherlands population probably rose equally rapidly and was more likely nearer three-quarters of the figure for England than three-fifths.[29]

In technological skill, productivity and national wealth, the importance of the Netherlands was even greater than the figures of size or population would suggest. For if war devastated and drained the south of its human skill and energy, the north seemed positively to thrive on its troubles. After the Treaty of Cateau-Cambrésis in 1559 its shipping, population and towns all grew rapidly. Let us return to the dialogue quoted earlier:

Q. Methinks Warre should undo them?
A. Of all the World they are the people that thrive and grow rich by Warre, which is the World's Ruine and their support, so strong is their shipping, so open their sea, so fortified their Towns and Country, by reason of their Lownesse and Irrigation.[30]

My reason for presenting this subject for Ford's lectures is precisely that it was in the Netherlands that a decisive chapter of English history was written between 1572 and 1609. The course of events in the Netherlands was not shaped merely by geography or topography. The survival of England as we know it was not merely the consequence of English valour and resource; nor was the survival and emergence of the Dutch Republic achieved solely by Dutch determination to govern their own destiny. As Trevelyan once wrote, 'the Armada would not have been defeated, nor the Elizabethan régime saved in England, if Holland had not first been saved in its last extremity by the relief of Leyden.'[31] The course of events in each area was inextricably entangled with the course of events in the others. The demands of the French wars on Spanish commanders at crucial moments, the recurrent crippling mutinies, deaths of commanders and the accidents of genius all helped to shape the course of the Revolt. In subsequent lectures we shall see how Elizabeth's policy, compounded alternately of snap decisions and the indefinite postponement of any decisions at all, of offers made, accepted, only to be withdrawn, was itself part of the unending play of contingencies.

Halfway through this Eighty Years War, some lines were written upon another tragic theme. They spoke

> Of accidental judgments, casual slaughters,
> Of deaths put on by cunning and forc'd cause,
> And in this upshot, purposes mistook
> Fall'n on the inventors heads. . . .[32]

Horatio's vision of a random world, out of joint and ruled by chance, could as well be drawn from the Netherlands as from an imaginary Denmark or an actual England. The play of contingencies in the Netherlands presented a constant challenge to Elizabethan diplomacy: a Netherlands where only the assassination of the Prince of Orange saved a reputation at its nadir, where Parma's brilliant victories merely led him into the abyss, where Antwerp, the hinge of success or failure, might have been preserved if English help had arrived in time. The sixteenth century was nothing if not casual.

2 International Peace and Civil War

LITTLE more than three months after she became Queen, Elizabeth dispatched Sir John Mason to Cateau-Cambrésis. His mission was to pour out the vials of her wrath upon the English Commissioners desperately trying to negotiate England out of the war. They had committed the unforgivable offence of allowing the French to question the Queen's title and to refuse to return Calais. The effect was evidently traumatic. Even Mason was touched by the distress into which the Commissioners were plunged: 'Poor Doctor Wotton* was fallen into an ague of mind.' Another Commissioner, the Bishop of Ely, Thomas Thirleby, a Polonius-like figure who, with much wringing of hands, had sold his old friend Thomas Cranmer into perdition, was 'factus totus stupidus'. 'The senses of her Ministers', Mason reported, 'are taken away by sorrow.'[1] But it was too late to do anything. As the Commissioners had mournfully declared in Mary's time, 'poor England that begun not the fraye' was doomed to lose her 'jewell'.[2] So Calais was lost. And it was lost because Philip of Spain was not prepared to allow the English claim to Calais to obstruct a speedy peace with France. There was no open breach, but Spain's coolness and Elizabeth's rejection of Philip's advances over a marriage had left an unmistakable chill in the air. Sir Thomas Chaloner, her agent in Brussels, reported to the Queen that the Spaniards in the Low Countries were hostile to England. Philip and Granvelle, his spokesman in the Netherlands Council of State, were giving them the lead, 'though still dissembling'. In contrast, 'the gentilmen of theis low partes . . . take our parte and canne not endure to here us yll spoken of.'[3]

By the end of 1559 the pattern of discord was becoming more and more complicated. The States-General were at odds with Spain over taxation, the presence of Spanish troops and Granvelle's reorganisation of the Netherlands bishoprics. The phase of revolt by the high nobility was beginning, and to their grievances in the mid-sixties were to be added the more violent protests of the League of the lesser nobility. Even in 1559, Chaloner complained of the extreme dearness in Flanders of 'wood, wyne, brede,

---

* Nicolas Wotton, a sensible if unlearned cleric and an experienced diplomat.

extraordinaries and howserome . . .', which shrank distressingly the value of his salary.[4] Everywhere, as inflation took hold, economic distress increased the appeal of the more emotional forms of Protestantism to the lower orders of society. Hence in part the outbursts of image-breaking, violence and destruction.

Domestically, by 1565–6 inflation, hysteria and panic were all at work, especially among the wage workers, and they now included the skilled craftsmen. Externally, the Council of State had done nothing to stop the downward drift of relations with England. On the contrary, the sale of arms to England was prohibited and rumours spread that France and Spain were contracting an alliance against Elizabeth.[5] The Queen might protest her fervent desire that the old alliance with Burgundy against France should be renewed. Philip turned a deaf ear. Something like an economic war set in. The Flemish merchants denounced England for breaking the *Magnus Intercursus* and for attacking Flemish and Dutch ships and fishermen.

So far from bringing peace to Europe, the Treaty of Cateau-Cambrésis had merely substituted one kind of sword for another. The confrontation of the major powers on the battlefield might have ended for the time being; a new phase now opened and it was dominated by the spy, the assassin, the *agent provocateur*, the Fifth Column, the privateer and the pirate. In England, Spanish agents instigated and supported the plots and risings of the Roman Catholics; in France, Spain promoted the Guise faction. In the Netherlands, as the aristocratic opposition to Philip's centralising plans hardened, those nobles whose sympathies were Protestant looked to the French Huguenots for support. France herself was plunged into forty years of crippling violence and social chaos, during which she suffered, on a modest count, nine separate civil wars, down to the Peace of Vervins in 1598.

The phase sometimes called 'the revolt of medievalism' lasted approximately a decade – from 1567 to 1578. I shall dissect the structure of the nobility in my next lecture. Here I will only remark that even before the Revolt began there were significant differences between the social structures of north and south. In the north there were few great nobles, few great prelates and only one diocese: Utrecht. Gelderland and Overysel, with a numerous class of middling gentry, did not seriously invalidate this general principle. Compared with the great noble houses of the south, the

Croys, Lignes, and the rest, the nobles of the north wielded relatively little political power. The one real exception perhaps was Brederode, Lord of Vianen and owner of approximately one-twelfth of Holland. One of the Earl of Leicester's entourage sneered at England's allies of 1586 as 'Sovereign Lords Millers and Cheesemen . . .'. The jibe was supercilious but near the knuckle: this contempt for a meritocracy of tradesmen always hardening into oligarchy, an oligarchy based not on the nation or even the region but on the individual town – this contempt lay at the root of the hesitation, anxiety and repulsion that Elizabeth, Burghley, Leicester and others felt towards any equal alliance with the northern rebels.

Hardly less repellent did the Queen find the act of rebellion by the nobles of the south. Not until after the signing of the Treaty of Nonsuch in 1585 could she bring herself publicly to deplore the treatment of the leaders of noble opposition in 1568. To the protests of Egmont and Hoorne and the careful arguments of the Prince of Orange in defence of the rights of the nobility her ear was totally deaf. She remained unmoved by those of her advisers who pointed out that the King of Spain did not scruple to encourage rebels in her own territory. Probably she believed, as Cardinal Granvelle himself did, that the noble resentment was in reality directed against the Cardinal himself, and sprang from noble jealousy of a successful upstart family from Besançon, combined with the bankruptcy of their own class, which consistently lived high above its income. There was probably a measure of truth in this, as also in the Cardinal's further conclusion that Philip would do well to bribe the nobility into acquiescence. Parma was to prove that the nobility were eminently corruptible but by then there were few more honourable alternatives open to them.[6] The rebels therefore got short shrift from the Queen. She publicly approved the execution of Egmont. She promised to celebrate the downfall of Louis of Nassau, brother of William the Silent, with 'a feast, a bonfire and a *Te Deum*'.[7] An appeal by Count Hoogstraten, a Lalaing, for her intercession on behalf of Egmont and Hoorne went without acknowledgement.[8] The fact that the rebels were nobles, Knights of the Golden Fleece, Stadholders or occupants of high offices of state did nothing to excite her sympathy. Rather the reverse: their crime against their anointed sovereign lord seemed that much greater. Were there not other great lords – Aerschot, head of the great house of Croy, Aremberg, Havrech, Berlaymont, Viglius, for example, all Knights of the Golden Fleece – who smothered their personal dislike of Granvelle, and either joined heartily in the ruthless suppression of revolt or by at least abstaining from protest lent respectability to the proceedings of Alba's Council of Blood? As in other civil wars, the nobility here were deeply divided. Quite apart from her primitive, instinctive hatred and fear of rebellion, these divisions would have caused Elizabeth to reject the arguments of William the Silent's *Justification* of 1568. She had her own Norfolks, Nevilles and Percys and she knew their revolt was already ripening. The maintenance of authority must unquestionably take precedence over the inviolability of privilege. The rebels were betraying their sacred duty to the principle of 'degree'.

It would therefore be quite wrong to associate the Queen's next major undiplomatic move with any motive of sympathy for the Netherlands Revolt. In December, on the Queen's orders, ships carrying bullion to the Netherlands to pay Alba's troops were seized at Plymouth and Southampton, where they were sheltering from pirates. Some eminent authorities have seen this as an ingenious blow against Spain, a rare show of queenly resolution and decision.[9]

Was it? Whatever the legal rights and wrongs of the action, the Queen's precipitate action sparked off a crisis, the economic consequences of which lasted more than four years. And they were dire. The immediate reprisals fell again on the luckless Merchant Adventurers at Antwerp and elsewhere, who, along with their servants, were arrested. At Amsterdam fourteen of them were imprisoned in a single small 'foul and stinking cell, four feet wide and ten feet long'. The next month, January 1569, Alba placed a total embargo on Anglo-Netherlands trade. Elizabeth answered with her own reprisals. Forty ships from the Netherlands were arrested. True to form, Burghley gloomily began to predict war and defeat. Luckily Philip and Alba had their hands full, though the economic crisis unquestionably gave the Spanish Ambassador added excuse for supporting the northern rebels in England, the Ridolfi Plot, plans for an invasion of England from the Low Countries, and the rising in Ireland.

The countervailing measures made necessary by these threats were highly expensive. They included the muster of the militia, the distribution of armour and weapons in the threatened areas, and in the summer of 1570 the requisition of all ships over 30 tons for naval use. Trade with the Netherlands and Spain was totally disrupted, while the Customs were reduced by some £4000 – perhaps 6 per cent – for several years. In all, the loss of customs revenue and the outlay on defence probably cost over £180,000. The value of the treasure, which in the end had to be repaid to the Genoese bankers who owned it, was perhaps £75,000. On top of the cost to public funds there were the heavy private losses which followed. Exports of cloth fell to little more than half the figure of 1550. Another nail was driven into the coffin of the London–Antwerp trade as English merchants tried to divert their cargoes to Hamburg.[10] Once the dyers and finishers who treated the English cloth at Antwerp had been dispersed to Hamburg, Emden, Nuremberg and Stade, it was not easy to restore the economic *status quo* at Antwerp. Unwin seems to have been nearer the mark than the political historians. To him Elizabeth's action was a pointless act of piracy.[11] It was the first but not the last indication that the decisions that came most easily to the Queen on diplomatic and military matters were taken on the spur of the moment; and they were usually bad.

The possible argument in favour of her action is that she succeeded in creating serious financial embarrassment for Alba. But even this seems equally implausible. It is true that Alba could ill afford to lose even £75,000 at this juncture. But his immediate response was to press on with plans to raise enormously larger funds by means of the 10th, 20th and 100th penny. Even the grant-in-aid which was the practical result of his negotiations with the Netherlands provinces yielded sums vastly larger than the loss at Plymouth. The cost of the Netherlands war to Spain was already probably running at somewhere between two and three million escudos a year, or rather more than half a million pounds sterling.[12]

The most serious consequence for Alba of the Anglo-Spanish crisis may have been the loss of some 2000 brass cannon collected at Veere on the island of Walcheren, brought there in 1570 in connection with a projected invasion of England. Their capture was the work of the rebels.[13] Meanwhile the Anglo-Spanish rift continued until 1573, when it was finally resolved by a treaty under which Elizabeth tamely paid back everything she had stolen. So ended an escapade as costly as it was senseless.

By the time trade and something approaching amity were restored between England and Spain, the merchants and ports of almost the entire Atlantic coast had become familiar with the remarkable and often terrifying movement known as the Sea Beggars – the *Gueux de Mer*.[14] In 1572–3, a year of intrigue, violence, assassination, revolution and massacre in Europe, the Beggars played the decisive role in establishing by force the future of the northern Netherlands. A spontaneous movement composed of the extreme elements which had played an important role in the rebellions of 1566 and 1567, the Beggars had taken to the sea and steadily strengthened their grip on the entire western seaboard of Europe from La Rochelle northwards up to the Frisian Islands. Their leaders were minor nobles like William, Baron of Lumey de la Marck of Liége, a picturesque, bearded, tribal ruffian of ruthless ferocity who had sworn a solemn oath to avenge the execution of his kinsman Lamoral, Count of Egmont. William the Silent had harnessed their wild energies to his cause by issuing them Letters of Marque, which as a sovereign prince he was fully entitled to do.[15]

The early months of 1572 were utter confusion. Elizabeth was still playing fast and loose with Spain's envoys. Walsingham, her Ambassador in France, was still toying with Louis of Nassau's project to divide the Netherlands between France and England. William the Silent was addressing a new *Justification* to Elizabeth as an outraged feudal subject, a victim of Spanish tyranny, while the Flemish nobles were still defying Alba's demands for new taxes. Lumey was refitting his Beggar fleet at Dover where he had taken shelter. Alba (wrote Walsingham) 'beginneth very much to droope'.[16] But in March a sharp exchange took place. Lumey, an assiduous but unwelcome courtier of the Queen, who never stooped to the use of anything but Latin in his addresses, presented her with a particularly fulsome, rhetorical piece offering her the services of his fleet. He asked, in passing, that it might be allowed to use Dover freely. His reward was a peremptory order to get out. Early in March he went. Until 1 April he cruised between Dover and the Downs, hinting that he would in due course seize The Brill, a small but strategically placed port in a commanding position to the north of the delta where the great rivers crossing the Low Countries join the sea.[17] On All Fools' Day he made good his promise. Alba, said a message from Brussels, 'teareth the heare of his hedd and bearde'.[18]

The capture of The Brill, followed as it was by the Beggars' conquest of strategically vital ports and towns throughout Holland and Zeeland, was to prove the foundation stone of the Dutch Republic. It secured the western flank of the Revolt and gave it naval bases and access to the ocean, lifelines by which it was to be sustained. It meant that the rebel provinces were not merely an enclosed fortress in which the defenders might well be trapped to death, but a *place d'armes* with free access inwards and outwards for arms, supplies, food and men. But was it, as has recently been suggested, the result of the initiative of Elizabeth, 'an enterprise concerted by [Lumey] with the English Government under cover of expulsion'?[19] Certainly the movement of liberation came from the sea, but did it owe 'its initial impulse to Elizabeth of England', as Professor Wernham has suggested? As far as I can judge, Professor Black settled this issue for good and all nearly forty years ago. He pulverised the evidence which purported to show that Lumey departed for The Brill with Elizabeth's connivance. All these rumours, as he showed, rested on gossip from Spanish sources. Lumey had to cruise in the Channel for nearly a month, getting shorter and shorter of food and water until finally, in desperation, he fell on The Brill on 1 April. Elizabeth sent in no English or Scottish volunteers to Zeeland for another three or four months, and then only because the French were threatening to dominate the key port of Flushing. (Earlier volunteers were Flemings and Walloons from the Netherlands congregations in London, Norwich and Sandwich.) There is no mystery to be solved here. The truth is quite simple: Elizabeth ordered out the Beggars because they were highly unwelcome guests, and they went. She can claim no credit for their crucial victory.

Once The Brill and the other Zeeland ports (Flushing especially) were firmly in Beggar hands, the situation was very different. For Flushing controlled the channel through which the entire trade of Antwerp must sail. Who was to command it? Elizabeth was compelled to bring into play all her own endless resources of guile and double-talk, backed by the tortuous cogitations of Burghley. From a characteristically tight-rope posture, Burghley delivered his opinion: if Alba could cope with the rebels, England should keep out; if he could not, let Spain be told that England would help Alba provided Philip would 'discharge his subjects of their intolerable oppression, restore them to their ancient liberties, reconcile his nobility to him, deliver them from the fear of the Inquisition, etc.' This was the outline of policy which, according to an influential body of historical opinion, was consistently pursued by Elizabeth at least until 1585 and probably for the rest of her reign. Its justification is said to lie in the French menace which is supposed to have hung suspended over the Netherlands and therefore over England. For if Spain were driven out, would not France step in, especially since the House of Orange is supposed to have shared at any rate one inclination with its rival houses among the Walloon nobles: an unsubstantiated faith in the constancy of French policy towards the Netherlands?[20] Such assumptions neglect two important facts. First, the Burghley policy, which Elizabeth certainly followed, though less consistently than is often supposed, was open to the obvious objection that from Cateau-Cambrésis onwards Philip had not the slightest intention of implementing any policy of co-operation with the magnates in the old tradition of Netherlands 'liberties'.[21] For reasons of expediency his commanders might wish to postpone a reckoning with the dissident powers, Protestant or Catholic, who stood in Spain's path. But the infiltration, the bribes, the intrigues were unceasing. The Burghley policy, sincere or otherwise, was in reality merely a diplomatic formula for inaction, in practical terms meaningless. Second, the Queen and Burghley overestimated (or more probably found it convenient at times to seem to over-estimate) the strength of France. A France divided and devastated by civil war did not pose the threat they pretended to fear: if it did, why were they to show themselves ready on so many occasions to enter into alliances with France that would have made it far more serious? Or was all this elaborate shadow-boxing principally designed to save money and minister to Elizabeth's parsimony – a not unreasonable financial policy provided it was not merely putting off a much costlier day of reckoning?

For the moment the anti-French line seemed plausible. In the wake of the Sea Beggars, a French garrison and governor took over Flushing. And Flushing, on the south side of the island of Wal-cheren, commanding the main channel up to Antwerp, was the fulcrum upon which the strategy and diplomacy of the next few years turned. Treading hard on the heels of the French came a small expeditionary force of English volunteers under Sir Humphrey Gilbert, the navigator, Thomas Morgan, a Welsh soldier of fortune of gentry stock, and another Welshman destined for later renown, Roger Williams. One of Gilbert's company commanders at Flushing, Thomas Cotton, put the situation concisely. There would be great advantage, he wrote, in England's possessing Flushing and Middelburg, for thus one could control a great part of European trade from Scandinavia south to Spain. On no account should France be allowed to have it. Meanwhile the Queen herself reminded Gilbert that his major task in Flushing was to contain the French, adding in characteristic *sotto voce* that she could look to his 'soe demeaning himselfe as though he and his companies departed out of England thether without Her Majestie's assent'.[22]

Gilbert was immediately shut out of Flushing by the French Governor, but in a touching episode the townsmen demanded that the English, 'their ancient friends and neighbours', should be allowed back. It was all done 'with such a general affection . . . as both teares were shedde and their own beddes presented to the Englishmen though they should lie on the ground themselves'. Improving this shining hour, Sir Humphrey dispatched a loyal and gallant message to the Queen promising to 'cutt all the Freynsse in peasses and the Governor also'.[23] Alas! his predictions were too optimistic, and the next few years were to see the goodwill of the Zeelanders evaporate as their frustration and disappointment with Elizabeth's shifting policies grew.

The next year, 1573, saw events sliding into total confusion. Gilbert was not a leader to inspire his men and was soon withdrawn. But the build-up of troops continued, albeit slow, hesitant and surreptitious. They were mainly Scots – 'idle men and soldiers' – originally ordered out of Edinburgh because of a prevailing famine. Here, on the ramparts of beleaguered Haarlem, the Scots Brigade had its inauspicious beginnings – Scots (as the Brigade's historian laconically remarks) being always regarded as 'mercenaries' while the English were always 'volunteers'.[24] By 1573 there were three companies in Dutch service under Colonel Ormiston. The Balfours, Pattens, Robesons, Erskines and Stuarts followed. By 1576 the Scots numbered perhaps 2000.* But the Anglo-Scots

---

* The Brigade, as it became, was a strongly family affair that survived in Dutch service until the American War of Independence.

contingent, ill-led, unpaid and unhappy, was too weak as yet to influence the course of events in Holland and Zeeland. Haarlem fell to siege; Mons was lost; the population of Naarden was massacred; Leyden was blockaded. The 'river defence line' offered little comfort at this juncture. The defensive, obstructive potential of the Dutch was enormous. What they lacked was an offensive spearhead, which only England or France could provide. But Elizabeth, seeing no hope in the Dutch cause, now tacked back hard towards Spain. The Anglo-Spanish Treaty promising an end to the economic war was signed in March. Those Protestant sea-dogs, Hawkins and Frobisher, were meanwhile negotiating to supply sailors for the Spanish service,* while the members of a Dutch mission dispatched to England on behalf of Orange were summarily jailed.[25] Burghley, gratefully acknowledging Spanish gifts for himself and his family, prepared to dispatch his agent, William Herle,† to try and persuade Orange to give up the unequal struggle[26] (even though reports put the Prince's public support at 10 to 1 of the population). The Queen rounded off the whole frenzied confusion by announcing to the Spanish agent in London that she would 'cheerfully hang any English in the service of Orange'.[27]

The outlook for Orange could hardly have been blacker. Yet his nerve was quite unshaken. When William Herle had an interview with him in June he found the Prince calm, eloquent and forceful. Courteously but firmly he asked Herle to impress on the Queen of England that the Netherlands were only Philip of Spain's first victim. If they were defeated, it would be England's turn next. With much skilfully deployed argument, economic and political, the Prince urged that the Queen should send help, not in defence of the Low Countries, but in execution of her duty as defender of the realm of England. Sensing the Queen's psychology, he then turned to the delicate matter of rebellion. The Netherlanders, he declared vigorously, were no rebels; they were loyal subjects who had been outraged in their traditional rights of freedom, consultation and property. It was Philip who had behaved shamefully and had not hesitated even to stir up revolt in England amongst great personages.[28]

---

* This episode is still obscure. The negotiations were certainly known to Burghley but the inference that it was never intended to implement them in practice is less clear.   † See p. 148 n. 66.

It was an eloquent and persuasive argument, designed to calm Elizabeth's fears about the rebels, to inflame her fears of Spain, of rebellion in England, to play on her ambition, her parsimony and her native caution.

William was well aware that he held few cards; but he did hold one. So long as he held on to Flushing he could look across a mile or two of the Scheldt estuary and block all trade into and out of Antwerp. Already the unhappy English Merchant Adventurers were petitioning at Flushing for free navigation of the Scheldt; but Orange was saying nothing. This was how matters stood when some changes in the dramatis personae took place in November. Alba, exhausted and bankrupt, wrote to his master on 17 November, 'kissing his feet' for giving him permission to return and hand his duties over to Don Luis de Requesens. A few weeks later Philip's move was matched by a complementary appointment by Elizabeth. Walsingham, recalled from France, was appointed principal Secretary of State. The Queen might not like Walsingham or his opinions: she could not ignore his ability. Thus almost simultaneously the ruthless military genius of Alba was removed from the Netherlands and the forces of Puritanism augmented in the Queen's counsels. De Guaras, the Spanish chargé d'affaires, had no illusions. 'This Walsingham,' he wrote, 'is of all heretics the worst . . . the right hand of Orange. . . .'[29] Two years later William himself declared that he regarded Walsingham as 'the chiefest friend he had in England'.[30] He was probably right but de Guaras was wrong. Walsingham, a Marian exile, a dogged Protestant, the smooth organiser of an intelligence service equal to that of Spain itself, certainly set himself to wean Elizabeth from her pro-Spanish conservatism. In this he had little success. He did, however, bring with him a new group of Protestant enthusiasts, who collectively worked towards an Anglo-Netherlands alliance and at the very least postponed the total breach that seemed to threaten. But if they favoured a Netherlands alliance it was because they believed that it was essential to the safety of England. A central figure in the network of personal and diplomatic links between England and the Netherlands which now developed was Daniel Rogers.[31]

Daniel's father, John Rogers, had been chaplain to the Merchant Adventurers at Antwerp, had become a Protestant convert and been burnt at the stake early in Mary's reign. His mother was an

Antwerper and he himself was related to some notable figures in the Netherlands congregation of the Dutch Church at Austin Friars, only recently presented by the Queen to the Dutch colony of London. Among them were Jacob van Meteren, printer, historian and antiquarian, Abraham Ortelius, the famous cartographer, and the Utenhove family, originally of Ghent, through whom the rhymed psalms in Dutch were first made available to the London Dutch Calvinists. Daniel Rogers first travelled to Paris as tutor to the children of the English Ambassador, Sir Henry Norris. When Norris was replaced as Ambassador by Walsingham, the new Ambassador soon became Rogers's 'especial frende and patrone', as he called him. In Paris he met the poet–scholar Jan van der Does (Janus Dousa), who with Jan van Hout was to lead the defence of Leyden a few years later. In 1572 Dousa visited England with an introduction to Burghley and an address to the Queen. Meanwhile, at Walsingham's house, Philip Sidney, Walsingham's future son-in-law and nephew to the Earl of Leicester, had met Dousa, Rogers and Hubert Languet, the intimate friend and adviser of William the Silent, him whom Rogers called 'my old Burgundian friend'. In 1574, on the day when the liberation of Leyden was celebrated by a pageant, Dousa, the most steady and unshakeable of the Leyden resistance leaders, put a Garter, not a Golden Fleece, round the crests of the Prince of Orange and the provinces on the decorated barge.[32] The gesture was contrary to the rules of heraldry, but it symbolised the hopes which had been expressed at Flushing and which were even now personified in a network of relationships between the Anglophile regents of Leyden like Dousa, van Hout and the Pensionary of Leyden, Paulus Buys; members of the entourage of William the Silent like Languet and Marnix van St Aldegonde; and Walsingham, Rogers, the versatile, brilliant Sidney and his friend and later biographer, Fulke Greville. Greville had already remarked the qualities of Orange which were to be remembered later in his rich and tangled prose. In Orange he discerned 'An outward passage of inward greatness. . . . Because there [in Holland] no pedigree but worth could possibly make a man Prince, and no Prince, in a moment, at his own pleasure.'[33]

For many years Daniel Rogers was to trudge backwards and forwards between London and the Low Countries on innumerable diplomatic errands. His abiding belief in the importance of his mission emerges frankly from a letter to his friend George

Buchanan, the Scottish humanist, whom he had known in Paris. 'I cannot express,' he wrote in 1576, 'how I have (these two years) tried to make the Queen take an interest in the Prince's cause.'[34]

The first mission to the new Governor, however, fell not to Rogers but to another Marian exile, Sir Thomas Wilson, who undertook the first of his two embassies to the Netherlands in the late autumn of 1574.* Wilson was a highly competent lawyer, already well known as an author for his *Arte of Rhetorique* (1553) and – better known to our generation – his *Discourse Upon Usury* (1569).[35] He was, above all, a devout Protestant who held clear, firm views about the Netherlands, an admirer of Orange and ardently in favour of English intervention on his behalf. A curious choice, it might be thought, to lead a mission to Requesens to try and settle the brittle problem of the Scheldt navigation to Antwerp. Walsingham evidently thought so too. 'Christ and Belial,' he observed gloomily, 'can hardly agree.' Yet on first meeting Wilson found Requesens 'mylde and modest'. If he had come earlier, things might have been better, Wilson thought.[36] But after a few more interviews the Governor's manner toughened. Already his nerves were feeling the strain of the confusion left behind by Alba – the debts, the unpaid troops, the proliferating mutinies. Both Requesens and Philip were in fact desperate at the state of affairs in the Netherlands. Yet there was no likelihood of peace, Wilson wrote, 'the pride of the Spanish government and the cause of religion being the chief hinderance of good accord'.[37]

But by April 1575 an Anglo-Spanish agreement seemed in sight. Both sides agreed not to harbour traitors, and the Spaniards were prepared to allow English ships into Antwerp provided they undertook not to benefit the rebels. But the agreement could have no practical effect so long as the rebels controlled Flushing, for Flushing controlled the Scheldt. In a rage of frustration, Elizabeth issued an edict proscribing Orange and his supporters and forbidding her subjects to help them. The Governors of the Cinque Ports were to forbid them entry, 'aide, succour or relief'.[38]

The calm resolution with which Orange received the challenge cooled Elizabeth's temper. This time it was Daniel Rogers's turn to go and try to settle the quarrel between Orange, the Flushingers and the English. But by now the Dutch were on their guard. They

* He returned in March 1575. His second was from October 1576 to July 1577. In that month he became joint Secretary of the Council with Walsingham.

too possessed both pride and guile. After brave and patient attempts, even Rogers was constrained to admit that they were 'kunninge masters of knittinge and inventinge of delayes' in suits at law.[39] The fact was that the worse the situation of the rebels became – and it deteriorated rapidly in the second half of 1575 – the more obstinate their resistance proved. The Spanish strategy was clear: a wedge was to be driven between Holland and Zeeland. If the Queen refused to help Orange, now proscribed, there was no alternative for him but to turn to France. Elizabeth's prevarications, Rogers reported, left him in despair.[40] Then once more as the year ended, the wheel began to turn again. Elizabeth was now thoroughly alarmed at the threat of a French alliance with the rebels, especially after 13 October, when the news came that the States of Holland had formally abjured the authority of Spain. On the other hand, the rebel cause seemed after all not irretrievably lost. Zierikzee, in the middle of the islands of the Zeeland estuaries, was still holding out, while an English agent in the area sent home an optimistic appreciation: 'The King's forces in these partes never weker, the hartes of the country never more alienated and the Governor mutche dismayed.'[41]

He was absolutely right.[42] Now it was Orange's opportunity to turn the screw. In successive interviews and messages he set out the attractions of a Netherlands alliance to England – the ports, the ships, the trade they could offer. He rehearsed all over again the historic rights of his Netherlands subjects which Philip had outraged. He showed that the Netherlands tradition of consent, so like that of England, was an insuperable obstacle to any peace with Philip. He hammered home the fact that it was Spain that had wrecked the Burgundian alliance of the Low Countries with England. Now the Spaniards were at a disadvantage while mutiny and disorder held the stage: now was the time to strike and give them a shock from which they would not recover. He ended with a stirring peroration: 'there resteth nothing but to resolve stoutlie and constantly and to take the occasion by the heare before she turn her back, when she leavith nothing behind but repentaunce.'[43]

Even Burghley, keeper of the Queen's conscience and the Queen's purse, now began to toy with the idea of a more decisive move towards Orange. His agents supplied him with mounting piles of intelligence about the Netherlands situation. Over these he brooded endlessly, setting out in characteristically laborious detail the possible courses of action and inaction. Relentlessly he indited a continuous stream of memoranda, partly in the hope of clearing his own mind, partly in the vain hope that out of all this repetitive, tedious and often confused abracadabra some miraculous formula might emerge which would solve all at a stroke of the pen. Was the future to lie with Spanish rule? A French alliance? English sovereignty? A union of England with Holland and Zeeland? What, he asked his Netherlands agents, was Orange's strength, especially in regard to the support of the nobility and the towns?[44] All these possibilities Burghley turned over and over through November and December 1575, while Zierikzee held firm and Requesens, now as bankrupt and distraught as his predecessor, became more convinced that peace must be made with Orange.

Orange had already expressed his satisfaction at the States' decision to make an offer of Netherlands sovereignty to the Queen of England, 'vû que la Reine faisoit de la foi Evangélique et descendoit des anciens Comtes de Hollande à quoi il faut ajouter l'opportunité de commerce'.[45] Now he was sufficiently encouraged to send a mission to England to seek the Queen's help. It was led by two of his closest friends and allies, Marnix St Aldegonde and Paul Buys. Discreetly, its composition hinted at his dilemma and his opportunities, for if Marnix, scholar and philosopher, was one of the leaders of Francophile policies in his entourage, Buys of Leyden was one of the foremost Anglophiles, a stout-hearted patriot, typical in his anti-Calvinism of the Erasmian, even *politique*, temper of the upper classes of Holland, fond of his bottle but brave and sincere.[46]

The mission left soon after the abjuration of Spanish sovereignty and carrying a proposal – possibly made by Marnix – that sovereignty should be transferred to Elizabeth as 'Lady and Countess of Holland and Zeeland'. It was certainly Marnix who drew up a family tree showing how the provinces might be shown to have descended legally to the Queen, together with encouraging precedents in favour of her legal intervention dating back to the time of Henry I.[47]

The Dutch mission found themselves faced with an extraordinary situation. Burghley had argued himself out of his usual auto-paralysis. Leicester was receptive to Marnix's approaches and Walsingham was known to be friendly to their proposals. In January 1576, therefore, the Queen's Council was united in favour of help. But the Queen's own reaction was immediate and electrifying. The divinity that hedged her royalty provided a special profusion of thickets and thorns against these commercial groundlings from the swamps and meres of the Low Countries, even when they came bearing what they supposed to be seductive gifts and offers. Resentful always of Walsingham, the only minister who ever succeeded in making her take decisions she disliked, she now augmented and transferred her resentment to his major colleagues on the Council. Gripped by one of those periodic fits of violent anger which were partly inherited from her father and partly perhaps attributable to her age (she was now 43), she locked herself away in her closet in paroxysms of hysterical rage, emerging only now and then to visit her fury on the Court and box the ears of those unfortunate ladies-in-waiting who happened to be nearest to hand.[48]

Yet the Queen's rage reflected not the weakness of the Netherlands cause but its strength. Her natural sympathy was with orthodox authority. These moods of violent desperation invariably overtook her when she was compelled to recognise that the interests of England coincided with those of rebels whom she instinctively hated. Thus the situation for Spain was critical as the anti-Spanish party in England continued to put pressure on the Queen to accept the legal force of Orange's arguments and to offer him substantial help, possibly even accepting the sovereignty of the Low Countries as well.

At this first critical juncture Requesens made an adroit move. On 12 January he dispatched to England the Baron de Champagny, Governor of Antwerp. The Baron, Frederick Perrenot, was the third brother of Cardinal Granvelle.[49] (The second brother, Thomas, had been appointed Governor of Antwerp but died before he could take up office.) Champagny was a smooth, enigmatic, elusive manipulator, who was to be in the wings of the political stage from this time until his death in 1602. Only occasionally did he emerge from his labyrinthine intrigues into the limelight. His most recent biographer has acquitted him of the Machiavellianism of his eldest brother and has suggested that his life was guided by his devotion to Church and King and his patriotic hatred of the Spaniards. Contemporaries did not all share this view. Paul Buys immediately scented trouble, impressing on William Herle (for his master's ear) that Champagny was 'as great a monster as Vitelli' (Alba's Italian lieutenant, who was so corpulent that he travelled everywhere with his enormous stomach supported in a large sling bandage). Herle discreetly muted down Buys's vignette to a message to Burghley that Champagny was 'a connynge and diligent fellow'.[50]

Champagny reflects the dilemmas, the cross-currents, the political passions of these years. A product of Habsburg state-making, he was born in Spain but he was no Granvelle. He was anti-Spanish, a loyal Burgundian but too much an *arriviste* to stand altogether comfortably inside the noble circle. He was also exceedingly brave, and one of the few truly devout Catholics in high politics. But his devotion to the Church (as to the King) was probably explained by the fact that both were abstract and remote enough not to provoke in him the waspish jealousies and thwarted ambitions which marred his relations with everybody else from the Prince of Orange to the Prince of Parma. Like others before and since, Champagny's inflated ego found that distance lent enchantment to a good cause. Causes nearer home were more easily resisted.

Champagny's first reception at the English Court was chilly. With Walsingham he was at once daggers drawn. Elizabeth had by now been reluctantly but distinctly softened by the arguments of the Dutch mission and the Privy Council, and Champagny warned Requesens that English opinion, including the Queen's, was upset by the reports of the bloody insubordination of Spanish troops in the Netherlands which was to culminate in the horrors of the total mutiny of Spanish troops that blackened the autumn of the year. Indeed if Champagny is to be believed, Elizabeth had already made up her mind, just before he arrived, to take Holland and Zeeland under her protection. Although this may have been something of an exaggeration, designed to throw into relief the magnitude of his task and therefore of his achievement, it squares more or less with the general trend of events as we know them. Hampered by his inability to decide anything without reference to his master, Champagny nevertheless set to work like the wily and tenacious negotiator he was. He was able to exploit effectively[51] the widespread indignation in London at the barbarous depredations on English shipping by the Flushing privateers. By the time the first round of talks ended, Champagny had won back valuable ground. The Queen retreated into her familiar position as pseudo-mediator between Philip and his subjects. The Earl of Leicester, seeing which way the wind was blowing, beat a prudent retreat and was clearly preparing to ditch his Protestant allies.

A second round went even better for Champagny. The Queen lavished all her charms and hospitality on him. Gresham provided a sumptuous banquet at which Elizabeth invited him to dance with her, 'ce qu'il a refusé avec bonne grâce et modestie'. Possibly he was alarmed by the intimidating vigour of the Queen's dancing, which was remarked upon maliciously by her enemies. After the party Leicester and Sussex accompanied him home to his lodgings. By contrast the Dutch mission, still patiently waiting on the condescension of comparatively minor functionaries like William Herle,[52] were subjected to unprecedented threats and insults. 'La Reine,' St Aldegonde wrote home gloomily, 'se laisse importer par sa colère. Là où nous espérons le salut, là sera la cause de nos désastres.'

While the Queen raged against the Zeeland pirates, the Governor of Zeeland threatened to close his ports against the English lest their ships should prove to be Trojan horses filled with Spaniards. To crown his apparent triumph, Champagny agreed to ask Requesens to withdraw the Spanish troops from the Netherlands, a move calculated to gratify the Queen as much as it enraged the Spaniards, who were now more than ever convinced that Champagny was double-crossing them. They were probably right.

The shabby treatment of the Dutch mission was not wholly due to Champagny's diplomacy. When Elizabeth trimmed, her mood usually reflected the state of the military barometer. This could hardly have been lower than it was in the Netherlands in the early months of 1576. After a dogged winter campaign, Zierikzee had finally capitulated to the Spaniards: thus the link between Holland and Zeeland was broken. Two of Orange's most valuable commanders were killed in the action, the Admiral Louis de Boisot and his brother Charles. Then in a dramatic flash, when this crucial strategic point seemed lost, the entire situation was suddenly transformed. Daniel Rogers, on a mission to William the Silent, reported Requesens 'dead of the pest' on 5 March.* At once the mutinies of Spanish troops spread, and the great loyalist nobles, led by the Duke of Aerschot, formed a Council of State to carry

---

* The diagnosis is more than doubtful. It seems more likely that it was some kind of malignant skin tumour. Requesens's had never been a good life and his health had been undermined by the continual anxieties of office.

on the government or, more accurately perhaps, to prevent the Netherlands relapsing into total chaos. Rogers saw little chance of improvement. The general mutiny of Spanish troops continued. Spain, he thought, would sooner lose the Low Countries and precipitate general chaos than recognise Protestantism, 'wherefore I see not how any peace may be made . . .'.[53]

In England, against all Walsingham's pessimistic forecasts, Buys kept up his spirits and went on talking to Herle. He put his trust in the 'wisdom and virtue' of Burghley, but he could not help recalling a trifle bitterly how things had changed since the Queen's original welcome, now soured by the delays, prevarications and worse that had followed. 'The Scottish faction,' Buys declared, 'lives on . . . advancing that bosom serpent the Scottish Quene.' Events in the Low Countries could well play into her hands. Requesens's successor might well prove a more dangerous threat: 'Many and dangerous be the partes that may be played upon the playn song of Don John of Austria. . . .' There were 60,000 men in arms there against Spain. Surely the Queen could see the advantage of taking action *now*?[54]

Buys's faith in Burghley and the Queen did more credit to his heart than his head. More sceptical observers regarded Burghley as 'the only lett and overthrowe' of the Holland mission. Walsingham had always told them they would gain nothing and merely lose their time. But Buys remained stoutly Anglophile in an Orange camp increasingly inclined to turn to France for help if the Queen would not budge. He might have been less trusting had he known that Burghley was at this very moment cautioning Herle not to be too intimate with Buys, while Champagny had formed a conviction that that other prop of the Continental Protestants in the Privy Council, Leicester, was at heart anti-Puritan, anti-Calvinist and pro-Spanish.[55] Yet both Burghley and Leicester were outwardly protesting their 'earnest and inward affectyon' to the Hollanders in general and to Buys in particular. Really the English were very perplexing! With almost excessive charity, Buys concluded that Burghley had done his best but 'God determines otherwise.'[56]

In the Scheldt, meanwhile, things went from bad to worse. The Flushingers held firm to their rights to tax English shipping to keep their war going – or if necessary to block all their trade to Antwerp. By June Anglo-Dutch relations were once again critical. £200,000 worth of English goods were held at Flushing, and when

Sir William Wynter* was dispatched to try and negotiate their release, Elizabeth told him to make it plain that she would expel every Dutch refugee from England and if necessary go to war to obtain restitution. This was diplomatic bluster. Burghley and the Queen knew perfectly well that there could be no question of an alliance with Spain. The defeat of Orange would lead straight to a Popish England and on its throne would be seated Mary, Queen of Scots. Burghley at any rate knew very well that the only course was to continue to negotiate with Orange. Orange, placatory but resolute, had his order of priorities: he was not prepared to waste time in an endless and pointless game of chess with the Queen while vital things remained undone – the revictualling of Zierikzee for example.

By the summer of 1576, even Elizabeth was again prepared to help the Prince, though troubled by the fact (as she remarked with regal distaste) that Holland and Zeeland could find 'only townesmen' to represent their case to her. Testily she continued to demand that 'a speedie and convenient plaster were applied to this corrosive sorre' (the clashes over the Scheldt navigation in and out of Antwerp). After all, Orange must realise that 'when all is done, England and Englishmen must doe him good and help him or ells he is utterly undone.' Strange doctrine this seemed, even to the Queen's agents in the Netherlands like Captain Edward Chester, let alone William the Silent, Buys and the rest. If only the Queen *would* help (Chester wrote to Burghley) 'she would find the hole countrie of Holland and Waterland at her owne devotion . . .'.[57]

Such was the tangled confusion of the late summer of 1576 as the Spanish mutinies reached their bloody climax – the Queen torn between a reluctant anxiety to help Orange (as a lesser evil than those which threatened from France and Spain), a still more compelling fear of the costs that effective help might entail, and an instinctive, visceral dislike of rebels, whether they were *seigneurs* or shopkeepers. How much more agreeable it had been to deal with Champagny than with these exigent, graceless tradesmen! Walsingham, sceptical as ever, had no illusions. To William Davison, who had been sent to the Netherlands to see how the new Council of State was getting on, he had already written in April.

---

* Wynter came from West Country seafaring stock. He was a fighting admiral and naval administrator of vigour and ability and an outspoken critic of what he regarded as the extravagance and corruption of Hawkins.

Davison had better come home. To stay was pointless. It would achieve nothing. There was 'neither courage nor other merit' in the Netherlands nobility except in Orange himself. They were not interested in their own liberty and they were prepared to make war on Orange 'out of common jealousy' with more extremity than the late Requesens himself. Besides, he ended bitterly, it was 'too publykely known that Her Majestie meaneth not to be a dealer'.[58]

3 The Queen, the Prince and the Crisis of the Nobility

REQUESENS dead, authority passed temporarily to the new Council of State, headed by Aerschot, head of the great House of Croy. But the Council was utterly inadequate to the task of restoring order and suppressing the Spanish mutineers, who were spreading chaos wherever they went. Even amongst the nobles, few were comforted by the announcement from Spain that the new Governor was to be Don John, victor of Lepanto, Philip's bastard brother. The explosion was predictable. A strong party of Brabant nobles – Guillaume de Hornes, Lord of Hèze and Jean, Marquess of Bergen, flanked by a number of abbots and town dignitaries, launched a new aristocratic protest. Hèze arrested the Council, while the States of Brabant summoned a meeting of the States-General, which added Flanders and Hainault to the revolt. It was still a mild, ostensibly limited protest, designed to restore order and give back to the nobility their proper place in government; its character was advertised clearly by the restoration to its leadership of the Duke of Aerschot, a pusillanimous booby devoid of brain or character.[1] His only act was to pledge the movement to the service of the Church and the King. Yet by 3 November, when the Spanish Fury fell upon Antwerp, representatives of the States-General and of Holland and Zeeland were already in discussion at Ghent. The news of the terror of the next few days, when some 8000 people were massacred (more than in the St Bartholomew massacre) and millions of guilders of damage done, changed the character of the movement from a neutral into a positive one. Urged on by the eloquence of Orange, the provinces drew up the famous document which came to be known as the Pacification of Ghent. The essence of the Pacification was that it united the most powerful provinces of north and south on an anti-Spanish platform. Orange was recognised in all his old offices and there was to be religious peace based on the *status quo* and no proselytising.[2]

The news of the revolution was jubilantly received in London. With the great nobles, including Aerschot, back in the rebellion, the leadership of the mid-sixties seemed to be restored: 'the chief doers,' ran one optimistic dispatch, 'are the nobles and gentlemen of all the Estates, M. de Lalain being a great doer therein. . . .'[3] Thomas Wilson was once more dispatched to Brussels to find out the facts. Meanwhile the new Governor arrived, the Spanish troops were ordered to leave, more provinces joined the States-General and a Union was signed at Brussels in January 1577, by which nobles, abbots and town deputies pledged themselves to the Pacification.

The next three years, between the Pacification and the formation of the Unions of Utrecht and Arras in 1579, between the fragile but genuine unity of the former and final division of the Netherlands by the latter, were a political and military watershed in European history. What was at stake was not merely the future of a sizeable territory and the most advanced economy of the contemporary world: it was the future of Europe itself for the next three centuries. For the preservation or destruction of the unity of the Netherlands was a key to the major problems of international relations in Europe – the relations of Spain and the great powers in the sixteenth and seventeenth centuries, of France and the great powers in the seventeenth and eighteenth centuries, even of Germany and the great powers in the nineteenth and twentieth centuries. This is the wider context in which we must look at Elizabeth's policies in these crucial years.

The central figure in the dramatic changes of fortune early in 1577 was William the Silent himself. The nobility were divided on principles, on strategy and on tactics. Many were easily drawn to agree to the so-called Perpetual Edict with Don John. Its object was the restoration of the old religion throughout the Netherlands. It made no provision for the States-General to discuss this and Holland and Zeeland were not consulted. With their usual unimpressive indecision, the States-General wobbled from side to side over the Pacification; but otherwise they gave Don John small cause for satisfaction. Aerschot, who symbolised all the pent-up jealousies of the House of Croy for the House of Nassau, was as unreliable as the rest. Hardly any of them wanted to make war on Holland and Zeeland. Though Catholics, they were mostly *politiques*, concerned first and foremost with their family affairs, their own estates and their own pockets.

By July the Governor's patience, never his strongest suit,

cracked. In desperation he and his bodyguard shattered the uneasy peace by seizing the citadel of Namur. Henceforth for half a year there was civil war, with the nobility confronting the King's deputy. Until the battle of Gembloux, an embryonic Netherlands state was in being.

Nor was there any doubt who was its head. From late in 1576 until mid-1577, William's authority grew as one after another the nobles, town magistrates and even the high clergy recognised the need for leadership and unity against the Spanish mutiny and the prevailing chaos. Philip, the young Count Egmont, was said to be the leader of a group of nobles 'bien affectionnés et voluntaires' which included Philippe de Lalaing, the Lord of Hèze, Glymes, Bossu and even Champagny.[4] Count Rennenberg, also a Lalaing, was protesting his deep friendship for Orange.[5] It was now Count Bossu's dearest wish that the States would come to a complete agreement to give full powers to Orange, 'estant chose si très nécessaire pour le bien et repos commun'.[6] Roels, Pensionary of Louvain, was at one with Olivier van den Tympel, a Brabant noble and future Governor of Brussels, and with John of Nassau in seeing Orange as the one man who could reduce the confused machinations of the senior nobles and the indiscipline of the younger ones to order. There were in the States-General, wrote John of Nassau, 'few patriots, many priests and young lords without experience, venal men, avaricious, ambitious, timid and pusillanimous men'.[7]

From Ghent, Count Philippe de Lalaing wrote moving tributes to Orange. Everyone, he assured him, depended upon him. There was no one else, 'de sorte que toute leur espérance resortit en vous, aiant ferme asseurance qu'avez et le vouloir et le pouvoir d'y donner ordre requiz'.[8] Even Aerschot was still assuring Orange, until late in 1577, of his 'singular affection . . . sincerity . . . fraternal devotion', and signing himself the Prince's 'most affectionate brother and cordial friend'.[9]

Orange's prestige reached its peak in the summer of 1577. On 17 September, and according to his usual custom unaccompanied by any bodyguard, he arrived at Antwerp. A week later he had a tempestuous reception at Brussels, jammed by welcoming crowds and decked with flowers. Aerschot rode beside him with other leading nobles. The scene seemed to bear out Daniel Rogers's earlier assurances to Walsingham that the Prince 'was generally

favoured of the people in Brabant and especially by them of
Brussels, besides sundry of the nobility which are at his devotion'.[10]
Behind the façade, however, the old jealousies festered. If money
and support for Orange were not to be forthcoming, it would not
be long before they once again broke out to destroy the fragile
unity which had been achieved. Now, if ever, was the time for the
Queen to decide and act. Before considering the potentiality of
English policy to influence the actions of the nobles and their
relations with Orange and Spain respectively, we must look more
closely at Netherlands society, especially in its upper reaches.

The dominant ruling class throughout the Netherlands consisted predominantly of the great Walloon French-speaking
families. The outstanding exceptions were the Orange-Nassaus, of
German origin, with possessions spread through France, Luxembourg and Germany but in the Netherlands mostly concentrated
in Brabant (round the palace at Breda); and in Holland and
Zeeland the Egmonts, originally of a Holland and Gelderland
family, who had married into the south. The Mansfelds were also
Germans. But for the rest – the Croys, Lignes, Brimeus, Montmorencis, Lalaings, Glymes, Hennins, Lannoys, Berlaymonts –
these and many more were Walloons, though their possessions
extended into Brabant, Limburg, Gelderland and sometimes into
Holland and Zeeland. Their individual names were frequently
taken from the Dutch names of their estates. The Duke of Aerschot
was head of the Croys, Aremberg (Stadholder of Friesland and
Groningen) was a Ligne, Meghen (Stadholder of Gelderland) a
Brimeu, Hoorne a Montmorenci, Rennenberg a Lalaing, Bossu a
Hennin; and so on.[11]

These great nobles – I will deal in a moment separately with
Orange – lived in high state, still perambulating like medieval
princes from province to province, from country to town house.
In the early period of the troubles their roots were mostly still
deep in Hainault, where a group of several hundred great and
minor nobles still accounted for over half the feudal incomes of the
province. Many were really quite small men – *chevaliers, écuyers,
seigneurs* they might be, but in reality they were more like early
Netherlands precursors of Macaulay's country squire. Their
affairs were on a different plane from those of the score or more of
great Walloon nobles, whose clients they often were. Hainault
especially was the home of the Croy clan – Aerschot, Chièvres,

Roeulx, Chimay, their relatives the Lannoys, the Lalaings, Hennins, Lignes, etc. Some had a foot in the towns and a stake in the town economies, as the Glymes did at Bergen-op-Zoom. The fact caught the eye of an acute Bohemian observer travelling in the Burgundian Netherlands in 1467.[12] But probably the largest part of the income of the group as a whole was from land. The loyalty of the class had been seen to be indispensable by the Burgundians. The Order of the Golden Fleece, an exclusive international club for the noble orders, had been founded by them to bind its members, Flemish, Walloon and Dutch, to the House of Burgundy. But aware that men live by rewards as well as honours, the Burgundians had cemented relations (as they thought) by lavish grants of land, pensions, and jobs in the Army and at Court for the great lords and their families. A proto-Namierian network of influence grew and the great Walloon houses waxed prosperous on the proceeds of Burgundian taxation.[13] Yet the objective of binding the nobility to the monarchy was only doubtfully and partially successful. When Habsburg succeeded Burgundy in 1477, the older ducal families already showed some animus, even joining hands with the citizens of Flanders against the new sovereign. Even newer families, like the Bergens and the Nassaus, Brabanters rather than Flemings, helped to wean Philip the Fair away from Habsburg dynastic objectives and educate him to be a Netherlander. A prime mover in this strategy was the great-uncle of William the Silent, Engelbert of Nassau.[14]

This Netherlands nobility was a large group comprising many different ranks. Below the great houses was a group, many times larger, of minor nobility, many really squires or gentlemen rather than nobles. They were *relatively* more numerous in the north, certainly more influential, than in the south. These were the men, often poor, often younger sons, who made up a large part of the five hundred signatories of the 'Compromise' of 1566. Significantly, 100 came from Friesland, 70 from Holland, 50 from Namur, while Brabant and Flanders only sent 25 each. Alba had swiftly thinned their ranks. One hundred and fifty faced imprisonment, banishment or violent death in battle. Twenty-five were executed or burnt alive.[15]

Were their grievances economic rather than religious or political? It is impossible to say. Certainly after the Treaty of Cateau-Cambrésis there were fewer jobs in the cavalry, and

Granvelle's reorganisation of the bishoprics reduced the number of church appointments open to them. Life at home and at Court was becoming more elaborate and costly. Inflation, whether it was caused by increased monetary supply, demographic growth or increased government expenditure, sent up the price of wheat fourfold between 1500 and 1570; other commodities followed suit.[16] In an age which saw a movement away from rents in kind to rents in money, landlords in general probably suffered.

It is impossible to calculate the incomes of nobles and noble houses with any precision. The Prince of Orange was certainly the wealthiest individual by a long lead, with an income estimated at two-thirds of the King's properties in the Netherlands. Aerschot and Egmont probably came next but a long way behind. Then a fairly large group – Hoorne, Bergen, Brederode – with incomes a fifth or tenth that of the Orange-Nassaus. The higher nobility could obviously absorb rising costs better than the gentry unless, as in so many cases, their property was sequestrated for disloyalty. But the idea that economic troubles underlay their mutinous behaviour did not have to wait on Victorian theories of materialist motivation. Granvelle had his own economic interpretation of aristocratic discontents.[17] Their troubles, he argued, were financial. It would be perfectly simple for Philip to buy them off: an excellent investment in peace and quiet. 'I remember writing to Your Majesty some years ago', he recalled in 1573, 'that the principal cause of the first rebellions in Flanders was the nobles' debts which made them unable to endure equal justice, since in paying up they were deprived of income and reputation, and because of this they wanted to govern. . . .'[18] Orange's estates in particular (Granvelle told Philip) carried an insupportable load of debt; and who better placed to know the facts than Granvelle, whose brother had been for long steward to the House of Orange?[19]

The condition of the nobility will continue to be debated. Yet even if Granvelle's economic calculations were well grounded (as I think they were), and his estimates of their political results not devoid of argument, his totally cynical conclusions were not at this moment necessarily correct. Noble hatred of the Inquisition was genuine. Most of the nobility, high-living, loose-living if you like, believed in liberty, including a large measure of liberty of conscience. Erasmus was in part the shaper of latitudinarianism, in part shaped by it. What is loosely called the Erasmian tradition was older than Erasmus, and it was outraged by the new dogmatism imported from Spain and enforced by Spanish *tercios*. This was coupled, in the minds of the nobles, with a natural concern for their property and privileges. They saw both threatened by Philip's principles and practices. Yet their response to their situation was neither uniform nor constant. It would have been surprising if it had been. In the early stages of the rebellion of the mid-sixties, many of the great nobility had joined in the protest – besides Orange himself, Egmont and Hoorne (neither very firmly), Louis of Nassau, William's brother, Nicholas de Hames, Herald-at-Arms of the Golden Fleece, the Counts Culemborch and van den Bergh (Orange's brother-in-law), Brederode and many others. Yet many of the greatest, like Aerschot, head of the House of Croy, had suspended judgement and action. It was to be their characteristic posture. Others, like Berlaymont, Noircarmes and Mansfeld, soon adopted an attitude automatically and unthinkingly loyal – the stupid old Tory party of the Netherlands. Berlaymont joined Alba's Blood Council.

But for the most part the nobles were *politiques* and anti-Spanish. If it be argued that this was the consequence of their economic situation, it must also be explained why the town patriciate, equally *politique* for the most part, moved towards revolution rather than away from it; why Ghent, traditionally radical, Brussels, Antwerp and many other dissenting meeting-places in the end tamely gave in. In part, the answer must surely be supplied by the differing character of the physical capital of the different classes. Much of the prosperity of the north was to come from southern immigrants – over a hundred thousand workers, artisans, skippers, shipowners, weavers, manufacturers and merchants, and bankers great and small. They had one thing in common: they and their wealth were mobile. The artisan of Ypres or Hondschoote could pack his small collection of tools and household goods on a donkey-cart or barge and go – to Leyden or Haarlem or even to Sandwich, Norwich or Colchester. The merchant might have more propertied encumbrances, but it was relatively easy even for him to run down his stocks and take wing with cash or paper credits.

The landed nobility and gentry had no such choice open to them, and if our sympathies happen to lie with the rebellion, we should at least recognise the problems and sacrifices they faced in joining it. The greater part of their wealth was in land and build-

ings and to these they were attached by self-interest and sentiment.
This, together with the generally conservative temper of a class
that owed much of its position to monarchy, helps to explain its
often apparently pusillanimous indecision, its impressionability.
Many nobles seemed to be at the mercy of every wind that blew.
Aerschot's unedifying political contortions sprang partly from real
conservatism, partly from jealousy of the House of Orange, partly
from sheer stupidity. His end, after thirty years of time-serving,
was a hysterical screaming fit when told to serve under Fuentes,
the new Spanish Governor, exile in Venice and dying pleas to
Madrid for baksheesh. The enormous clan surrounding him, led
by his brother, the Marquis of Havrech, a would-be demagogue
and actual intriguer, with his son-in-law Aremberg and his son
Chimay, were no less pathetic a collection. They all changed their
coats in 1576: they had all changed them back again by 1579.
Many others did the same, but in the other direction. The Count
of Bossu (or Boussu) was Alba's lieutenant and acting Stadholder
to replace Orange against the rebels in 1572; he changed allegiance
by 1576 to become the leader of the patriots at the battle of
Rijmenant in 1578.

The Lalaings of Hainault, a tribe almost as large as the Croys,
were likewise divided. Antoine, the close and loyal friend of
Orange, was killed during Orange's attempted invasion of the
Netherlands from Germany in 1568. Count Rennenberg, his
brother, having first joined Orange, finally deserted him, taking
with him Groningen, of which he was Stadholder, and went over
to Parma again in 1580.[20] Other leading Lalaings, though generally
anti-Spanish, showed little more consistency. Orange's own
brother-in-law, Count van den Bergh, an original rebel, after a
long if not distinguished career ended by betraying Zutfen to Parma:
so that when Maurice of Nassau tried to lay siege to 's Hertogenbosch eighteen years later, he found himself threatened by a reliev-
ing force commanded by his own cousin, Frederik van den Bergh.
Old Egmont had walked to his scaffold praying for his sovereign.
By 1580 his son Philip was not only reconciled but a leading officer
in the Spanish army.

So, even more than in the English Civil War, the first forty
years of the Revolt saw the ruling class of the Netherlands divided.
With them, as in England, went their tenants and dependants,
who formed a major source of the private armies they led into the

service of the States-General or Spain. Different members of the same family fought on different sides. Many changed their coats. Rebels were reconciled, loyalists defected. Few fought with any ideological relish or religious fervour. If there was any gusto in their martial proceedings, it was the gusto of animal spirits, of blood sports and the chase. The nobles were, to an overwhelming extent, *politiques*. Most of them formed part of that large body of men and women more or less indifferent to the extreme doctrines of Rome or Geneva. The recognition of the existence and importance of this large group of indifferents is comparatively recent, and it has modified many aspects of the historiography of the Revolt. Only a major threat to their rights and interests ever succeeded in uniting them voluntarily in pursuit of a cause. They had united in the sixties against Granvelle and the Spanish policy of centralisation, militarism and compulsory taxation. In 1576 they came together again to combat the breakdown of law and order, to restore government and eject the Spanish troops. Now they faced no Alba; Requesens was dead; Don John was unloved and mistrusted; and there was now a noble leader – Orange.

The Revolt threw up a few interesting men amongst the Netherlands nobility, many physically brave ones, the occasional soldier-scholar (like Philip Marnix St Aldegonde), a few villains and large numbers of mediocrities whose collective motto was *sauve qui peut*. It threw up only one noble leader of genius. Amongst the dwarfs and pigmies bred plentifully out of the Croys, Lalaings and the rest, William, later called the Silent, of Orange-Nassau, stands like a giant. In 1576 he was in his forty-third year. He can hardly be for us the 'statue of spotless marble against a stormy sky' that he was for Motley. William was more complicated, more sinuous, tougher, greater than that: statuesque, spotless he was not. His most important quality was his capacity to grow in moral stature to match his responsibilities. Surprised through the accident of his cousin's death in the French wars to find himself at eleven years of age one of Europe's major princes, he grew up amidst all the high living of the Court of Charles V, sharing and relishing it to the full. He was not unusually brave. He felt no ostentatious urge to improve on the flexible morality of the society in which he moved. Yet he was acutely sensitive to injustice, intolerance and persecution. From 1560 to 1573 his character seems to have undergone a gradual but profound change as he realised the implications of Spanish plans for the Netherlands.[21]

The precise nature of William's personal religion remains debatable. What is certain is that his publicly joining the Calvinist confession at Dordrecht in October 1573 was the climax of a long and earnest process of self-examination. Dogmatic Calvinist he certainly was not. He wanted no monopoly for Calvinism, no theocracy. Like many of the town rulers who were to oppose his successors, he was an Erasmian, in some sense a *politique*. His conversion to Geneva made little difference to his standing with the Catholic nobility, nor to the theoretical possibility that they might accept his leadership. The common view of the legal and historical position of the nobility which they shared was more important than the religious dogmas over which they differed and which most of them could not understand. As *politiques*, all understood well enough the force of the *cujus regio* principle which their German contemporaries had successfully forced on Philip's father.

In these formative years William grew steadily in intellectual and political as well as in moral stature. The common touch came naturally to him. The one great noble who spent his private fortune on the Revolt, forsaking his great possessions in the south and the family palaces in Breda and Brussels, he was compelled to live simply in a comparatively small town house in Delft. Willy-nilly he now lived amongst the people. He knew how to make himself liked, and he liked to be liked. But not at the expense of principle: he was in no sense a demagogue. Not the least part of his greatness lay in his never exceeding his powers and never falling short of his duty. Wherever he went he talked naturally, without affectation, to the ordinary people, civilians, soldiers and sailors. He became, as William Davison told Walsingham, the *Pater Patriae*,[22] 'Father William'. He possessed above all that quality which in the Latin languages is called 'sympathy', the gift of drawing people to him for guidance, discussion and persuasion. It was in part a necessity forced on him by circumstances, by political and financial uncertainty, but steadily it became second nature to him, part of his innermost being. This instinct and habit of discussion became fused with what was best in the surviving feudal ethos to make him perhaps the only political leader of the age who could claim to be a statesman in the modern sense, distinct from the hereditary dynasts, despots and demagogues who surrounded him.

The difference emerges clearly from his utterances as reported by contemporaries. These closely resemble his official writings – the *Justification* (printed at Dillenburg, the family estate in Germany, in 1568) and the *Apology* of 1581. It is most often assumed that these were largely the work of other helping hands, a kind of sixteenth-century forerunner of a U.S. Presidential brains trust. Probably it is true that Jacob van Wesembeeck, the Antwerp dignitary, merchant and banker who was his close adviser in the early years, helped to shape the *Justification*. Probably Marnix St Aldegonde, Hubert Languet and Villiers helped with the *Apology*; and as Marnix was the close friend of Hubert Languet, Duplessis-Mornay and the Francophiles in William's circle, it is natural to see in the *Apology* the influence of the *Vindiciae Contra Tyrannos* published the year before and often ascribed to Languet or Duplessis-Mornay. But it does not follow that William simply employed a team of ghost-writers. Throughout his scores of statements, spoken and written, of his political credo, there is the visible development of an unmistakably highly personal theme. Year in, year out, William hammered away at that still predominant body of opinion that would not countenance wilful rebellion against a lawful prince, but might be persuaded to sympathise with a grievously wronged subject. In the Netherlands, as Fulke Greville observed, this wrong took the form of an invasion or summary dismissal of the rights of the feudal vassal. One of the important offices of William's friends and sympathisers amongst English ministers, ambassadors and agents was to convey his repeated statements on this point to the Queen; for eighteen years she refused to listen. An anonymous memorandum of 1576, probably by Walsingham but possibly at this date by Burghley, set out the typical argument. The powers of the Prince of Orange rested, like all political authority in the Netherlands, on *consent*. Until he binds himself 'he is in no wyse taken or acknowledged as lord of the sayd contre'.[23] This was the ancient tradition of the Low Countries, and it applied just as much in Flanders or Brabant as in Holland or Zeeland. These ideas emanated (I believe) from William himself, though they were developed no doubt in discussion with his friends and advisers.

Between these principles, with their odd mixture of the feudal, the oligarchic, even the democratic, on one hand, and the bureaucratic centralised dynasticism of Philip on the other, there could be no compromise. Between the rest of the nobles and William, on the other hand, compromise was far from out of the question, and in these three years was reached – temporarily. For the nobles too had a stake in the continued prosperity of the Netherlands, not least the prosperity of the Netherlands towns. It was already clear that the towns, in north Italy and the Spanish-dominated Netherlands, were the first victims of the escalating costs of Spanish dynasticism, the grossly swollen courts, the indiscriminate taxation, the bribery and corruption, the devastation of war, the pillage, mutiny and disease that followed in the wake of the armies. What Orange needed if he was to consolidate his leadership was effective help. It could only come from England or France.

Thomas Wilson had been sent back to the Netherlands just as the Spanish Fury was rising to its climax. Rogers was stationed there permanently, and in March 1577 Philip Sidney joined Wilson in a special mission to the Prince of Orange. The next eighteen months, so crucial to the future of the Netherlands, of England and Europe, are therefore richly documented. The evidence shows that once again, as in the winter of 1575–6, the urge to action on behalf of William was not confined to the extreme Protestant group in and around Elizabeth's Council. Others, including Burghley himself, were persuaded that the confrontation between a state as united as it was ever likely to be, and totally alienated from a Spanish authority now almost isolated, made this the time to strike.

At the end of 1576 the States-General had still been united in opposition to Don John, still determined to oust the Spaniards. 'They doe desire chieflie', wrote Wilson, 'the Prynce of Orange to take the whole upon hym, who is a man not onelie of the greatest credite, but also of the greatest valeur.'[24] He was 'a rare man, of greate authoritie, universally beloved, verie wyse, resolute in al thynges and voyd of covetousnes, and . . . not dismayed with any losse or adversitie, his state now beeinge better than ever it was'.[25] Wilson continued to urge upon the Council, including Burghley, the need to support Orange politically and financially. This was vital not simply because he was obviously the natural leader, but because he and the States were now in full agreement – 'beeinge united to the States, who are now as he is, and he as they are, there case al alike. And the whole beeinge joyned together can never bee charged with that, which particulare members dividinge themselves from the whole bodie, were like to feel by order of justice.' Without him the whole State would be 'putte in hazarde'.[26]

But even Wilson could not disguise that Orange had some dangerous enemies. One, he thought, was Champagny, who had shown great bravery in the attempts to defend Antwerp against the Spanish mutineers. 'His witte', Wilson confessed, 'no doubt is verie greate, and al thynges passe under his hands.' Yet he was not 'resolute'. Nobody did more to hinder the Prince's dealings, except the Duke of Aerschot and 'those of the Howse of Croye, who woulde rule themselves, yf they had witte and credite'.[27] Besides the fissiparous connections of the Croys, Orange also had to face the opposition of 'the preestes who doe hynder moste his good proceedings and feare him, lest their authoritie and credite shoulde decaye and fawle . . .'.[28]

As the winter ended the signs of opposition from 'the unlarned clergie and the symple nobilitie' – the backwoodsmen – became more marked. Neither wanted William or the Queen to have any authority. Yet William's authority continued to grow. The States-General had resolved that if the war against the Spaniards was renewed he should be Chief Governor; and to satisfy the ancient but still virulent jealousy of Aerschot, propounded a plan for a marriage alliance between Croy and Nassau. The Croy heir was to marry William's daughter, and William's son, still a hostage in Spain, should on his return marry Aerschot's daughter.[29]

Encouraged by the reports of William's growing prestige, even Elizabeth became a little bolder. When the States-General succeeded in making peace with Don John in March, she indignantly ordered Wilson to demand of them why they had done this without consulting William, considering the heavy burden he had borne for their liberties and remembering that he was a man of such rare judgement.[30]

The answer was, alas, only too simple. English hesitations and Madrid escudos were a fatal combination. The old jealousies amongst the Walloon nobility had begun to fester again, and Don John and the House of Croy had steadily injected more poison into the wounds.[31] Neither Rogers nor Wilson concealed his anxiety at the turn things were taking. Orange's former allies were deserting, wholesale bribery of the nobles was spreading, the governors of the towns were 'all espagnolised'. Yet Holland and Zeeland were increasingly strong and prosperous, and their devotion to

Orange was beyond question. Rogers had been 'with the Prince in his coach as he hath travelled from Alckmare to Horne . . . and have seene such honour and affection shewed unto him as they would not shewe the like to the King of Spain . . .'.

Wilson returned in July, disappointed and disillusioned. What had gone wrong? One thing only. The Queen had failed to support Orange at the psychological moment when he needed to counter-act the jealous feuds within the noble camp and neutralise the lavish bribery that was daily winning more adherents to the Spanish cause. '. . . if wee have been the cause of this trouble abrode', he told Leicester, 'and fedde the factions (as the world gevvethe it out) the policie is not good, because it is not perpetuale but temporarie and for a season, and in the ende the harme wil whollie fawle upon us that are the suspected maynteyners covertlie and underhand of all these foreign broyles and troubles. Better not deal than not go roundlie to work.'[32]

Cryptic but prophetic. What were these 'covert and underhand devices' to which he referred? William was at this time under strong pressure from Don John to join Holland and Zeeland in the general peace. Leoninus, an academic from Louvain, who had already been used as errand-boy on earlier missions from Reque-sens to William, was now busy again. The Spaniards and their growing number of noble supporters clearly hoped that Elizabeth would be persuaded to join in the pressure for a settlement. Poor Wilson was equally anxious lest their hopes might only too easily be fulfilled.[33] The possibility seemed already to be emerging that William's role might after all be confined to the defence and government of Holland and Zeeland. Elizabeth's mind was now set on the project for a league of Protestant Princes, in which William would participate. These were the subjects discussed by the Prince with Philip Sidney and Rogers in July when relations between the Prince and the English party (who saw him as the defender of England as much as of Holland) were closer than ever before. On 20 July Rogers broached the idea of the League to William as something very much in his interests. If he agreed to it, Rogers assured him, the Queen's favour would 'increase by degrees'. William, always alert for this kind of gambit, took the words 'in very good parte, saying he had allways herde how wise and circumspect a princess Her Majestie were, and that he did not doubt but that Her Majestie would at the lengthe understande the designes of her ennymies, provide duly for them and enter into a farther amity with her well-wishers, and so takeinge a cupe of wine, dranke unto Her Majestie's health and wished me good-night . . .'.[34] Alas! that these two masters of the art of diplomatic fencing never met in person while Elizabeth was Queen.* It would have been a momentous encounter.

Four days after Rogers had seen the Prince, Don John had carried out his *coup* at Namur, capturing the citadel with his body-guard in an attempt to gain control of the country. But that was as far as he got. Attempts on other cities – Antwerp especially – failed miserably. Don John was left stranded and discredited, appealing in vain to Madrid for more troops. Once again everything was back in the melting-pot. The States-General, though divided, swung back again to the Prince in indignation against this alien outrage. The diplomatic scene came to life again. Agents bustled to and fro. Aerschot's brother, the Marquis of Havrech, was dispatched to London, where all the talk was now of sending an expeditionary force under Leicester to help the States-General. William Davison was brought into play again. His commission was as typical of the Queen as Gilbert's at Flushing five years before. He was to perform a balancing act between Don John, the States-General and the Prince, but it was made plain to him that only the Prince was to be trusted.[35]

Meanwhile a characteristically farcical operation was being mounted. Six hundred soldiers, mainly Scots, were sent hurriedly to the Netherlands. By night they were secretly smuggled from one town to the next, putting in brief daylight appearances in the hope of creating the impression that there were many more of them than there really were. Once more the Queen and her leading coun-sellors, including Burghley, were unanimously behind William. Davison took up the burden of the tale made familiar by Rogers and Wilson. The message seemed at last to have gone home. Holland and Zeeland were vital to the defence of England. They and their Prince would, 'yf Her Majestie omitte not the present opportunitie, . . . be suche an encrease of Her Majestie's strength as from abrode she needeth lesse to feare any ennemye, having the means thereby to be master of the whole Ocean from th'one end to th'other; and trewly, My Lorde,' Davison concluded to

---

* They had met in 1554 when William visited England in the Emperor's service.

Leicester, 'he [the Prince] is the man Her Majestie must make muche of, and they ar the provinces she must not lose, yf she will sitt safe at home.' The emphasis on England's welfare may have owed something to tactical considerations in dealing with the Queen; but there seems no reason to doubt that Davison was principally guided by what he believed to be the logic and the facts of the situation.[36] The States-General were equally convinced that the Netherlands' future was best secured by throwing in their lot with England. The Queen was implored by Havrech, their ambassador and Aerschot's brother, to send the Earl of Leicester with an army, and (for the first time) certain cautionary towns were to be offered as security. William himself, following up Philip Sidney's representation of Leicester as his stoutest supporter in England, evidently backed these appeals, if he did not originate them. Havrech and his party received an unwontedly warm welcome and an immediate offer of £100,000.[37]

Even the cautious Burghley had painfully concluded that the Queen's only course was to keep the Prince 'in hart and lyf'. In a more than usually tremulous note to the Queen he explained that 'the States of the Lowe-Countrey are so devided that howe trust may be reposed on them, when one trusteth not another, I see not; marry, if it might be brought to pass by counsaile from hence that the Duke of Arescott and states might governe the countrey according to their libertyes, and the Prince have the rule of their martiale matters, this of all others were the surest waye; otherwise, while the States be in deliberation, it may be doubted that their overthrowe may happe.'[38] In Brussels even Champagny was still proclaiming himself the Prince's most intimate friend and admirer and protesting his resolution to stand by him to his last gasp.[39]

This was the peak of William's power. Never again was he to enjoy the combined support of the mass of the people and a substantial element of the nobility; never to be so close to an alliance with Elizabeth and to the presence of an English army. In the Netherlands, Davison was energetically canvassing the merits of Leicester as saviour of the cause, while simultaneously advertising the merits of the Prince to Leicester. 'In somme, My Lord, I knowe not in the world a man Her Majestie may buylde uppon if not uppon him, whom I take to be inferieur to no man in hartie devotion to doe Her Majestie service.'[40] Leicester was nothing loath. Her Majesty had promised him the command. It would be, he said generously, five or six thousand foot and a thousand horse.[41] At Court, My Lords of Warwick and of Huntingdon were behind Leicester and Walsingham, and no doubt steadying Burghley's faltering hand. As if to underscore William's national and not merely northern authority, he had been elected on 22 October Ruward (to all intents and purposes Stadholder) of Brabant, his own province.

None of this meant that the Walloon lords had in any way muted their jealousies. It was Aerschot and Havrech, Lalaing and Hèze, with the advice of the egregious Champagny, who had secretly invited the Archduke Matthias, the Emperor's brother, from Vienna as early as August. He was to be protector of the dynasty and the Church. The new saviour accepted with equal secrecy, slipping privily from his bed in his night-shirt and setting off for Cologne, much to the rage of his mother, who knew nothing of the plan. 'For his person', wrote Davison, 'he is not above XIX years of age; he is thought of nature least corrupt of all his brethren, of bringing uppe meane for a prince of his qualitie. In religion a papist but easy to be reformed with good handling.'[42]

But far from improving matters, Matthias's arrival only made them worse. The Queen was still full of verbal support for William; but without much more than that he could no longer control the forces of disorder and extremism. In Ghent, the traditional centre of radicalism, the Calvinist fanatics stupidly arrested Aerschot. Orange at once ordered his release, but the episode widened the gulf between the rebels and the nobility. In England, autumnal doubts began to replace the resolution of the summer. Burghley, never a firm supporter of action, resumed his endless debate with himself, covering and re-covering the diplomatic ground, producing more of those *mémoires*, of which he was past-master, in which he weighed the possible benefits of doing something against the more secure advantages of doing nothing, invariably concluding that while William and the Netherlands were indispensable to the defence of England, now was not the time to act. 'Rarely decided . . . and never lucid; . . . least of all in emergencies, when decision and lucidity would have been more valuable than any other quality': Motley's verdict was hard but not unjust.[43]

An outspoken critic like Knollys* might urge the national defence to justify action on Orange's behalf: 'The avoyding of Her Majestie's danger doth consiste in the preventing of the conquest of the Lowe Countries betymes.'⁴⁴ It was all to no purpose. The Privy Council was in no condition to cope with these new confusions. Scarcely had a treaty been concluded with the States than their army was annihilated in battle at Gembloux, about nine miles from Namur, on the last day of January 1578. Don John, with 20,000 seasoned veterans, was supported by equally distinguished officers including Mansfeld, Mondragon, Mendoza and one newcomer whose presence was crucial for the present battle, even more for the future: Alexander Farnese, Prince of Parma, future Governor of the Netherlands. The States forces, a mixed bag of German, Walloon, English and Scottish mercenaries, commanded by officers whose loyalties were as varied as the nationalities of the ranks they led – Bossu, Alba's former commander, Champagny, the old Sea Beggar Lumey de la Marck, Havrech representing the Croys, and many others. Alexander's cavalry carried the day. The Spanish losses were negligible. Gembloux was a shattering blow. It did not, as we shall see, mean clear or permanent victory for Spain or total defeat for the Netherlanders; but it crystallised the differences latent in the Netherlands camp and it sent the English government scuttling back to perform another set of those strange diplomatic quadrilles which were the normal pattern of its Netherlands manœuvres.

This was tragic, since the one hope that sustained the States camp now was the promised arrival of English help.⁴⁵ All that was forthcoming was an icy inquiry from the Queen. What had gone wrong at Gembloux? Was it true – it was – that Count Lalaing was really pro-French? Who would guarantee that help given would be properly used? Davison did his best to reply and pacify. One result of Gembloux (he argued comfortingly) had been to unify the States behind the Prince – this was not entirely true but it was arguable, especially as the news had now arrived of the *coup* at Amsterdam which brought that obstinate and important centre of loyalism over to the Prince. He had now made suitable dispositions

---

* Sir Francis Knollys, M.P. for Oxfordshire, Privy Councillor, Government spokesman in the House and Treasurer of the Royal Household, did not, in spite of his personal loyalty, mince his words to the Queen. He was a stout Puritan.

to defend the entire Brussels area; everyone lived in hope 'that Her Majestie will not nowe leave theme in the bryers'.[46] Alas! they were already in the briars and Her Majesty was in no mood to extricate them. The thousand horse of Leicester's imagination could well have turned the tide at Gembloux. For it was above all horse, and more horse, that had been needed for that battle in the open country. The Privy Council might be 'in earnest and dailie consultation what is best to be done' in the Low Countries. They might be unanimous – 'inclined to one course for H. Majesty's Safetye' (as Walsingham put it) – but everything depended on the Queen and whether 'it may please God to inclyne herself to embrace and followe the same'.[47] It did not. As February passed into March, it became clear that once again the Queen had backed down. Leicester, disappointed of his promised command, had 'nether face, nor countenance to wryte to the Prince, his expectation being so greatly deceaved'. He could only ask Davison to protest his love and goodwill to the Prince, explaining that after all he was 'only a subject and servant'.[48] The unfortunate Davison, doomed to spend his life a martyr to the Queen's ingratitude,[49] was driven almost distraught by her irresolution, which was now playing havoc with morale, making (as he kept repeating) the States 'more incertain in their actions than the tyme and condition of their affayres requireth'. He explained what he believed to be the strength of the Prince and the States time and again to Burghley, to Paulet (Ambassador in Paris), to Leicester and to Walsingham, always hoping that the argument would filter through to the Queen. The Spaniards, he argued quite correctly, had failed to follow up their victory at Gembloux. The States had taken advantage of the delay to put into a good state of defence all the numerous and potentially easily defensible towns and cities of the south. Thus the Spaniards were faced with 'having to expunge one towne after another, the least of a number whereof cannot cost him (Don John) less than half a yares siege with an infinite charge, loss of men and hazard of his fortune and reputation because (as men of warr are wont to saye) one good towne well defended sufficeth to ruyn a mightie army'.[50]

The real stumbling-block now was that the Queen had decided that there were other and cheaper ways of conducting the war. One was already to hand in the not very prepossessing person of Duke Casimir, son of the Elector Palatine, son-in-law of

Augustus of Saxony. Casimir might himself be brainless, but he carried a brain with him in the person of Dr Beuterrich ('the equestrian doctor' as Philip Sidney called him), who acted as his public relations officer. In this capacity he had managed to persuade Elizabeth of the merits of employing his master; and indeed his argument was convincingly reinforced by Casimir's eleven thousand troops, which included a strong force of cavalry. To Orange, Casimir gave his loyal assurance that together they would be 'but two heads under one hat',[51] though without asking, as Motley laconically remarked, what enrichment this intellectual partnership would bring to William.[52]

William, never more impressive than when delivering one of his measured reproofs to his capricious ally, gave Daniel Rogers a long interview on 24 March.[53] Methodically, mercilessly, movingly, he indicted the Queen for her irresolution in breaking promises which would not only have 'bounde the Lowe-Countries to her for ever' but would have been a more honourable policy than that which she had chosen to follow. Not once but twice she had promised to send English troops. Twice she had failed. If they had come, Don John would not have won the towns and victories he had. 'Now all the fault wilbe layd upon me (quote he) and thei which are myne enemyes wilbe glad thei have gotten an occasion to saie that if the Prince of Orange hadd not willed the Estates to depende upon the Quene of England, thei had receaved succour from other places, or otherwise provided for themselves. . . .'

Rogers did his best to defend the Queen, but plainly his heart was not in it. Really there was no defence. As William had said to Rogers, 'no faultes brought greater inconveniences in tyme of warre than the losynge of tyme.' Against the advice of all those most closely concerned and best informed – Burghley, Walsingham, Wilson, Davison, Leicester, Sidney, Knollys, Fleetwood, Rogers and many others – she had refused to act on the conviction she herself had expressed – that the leadership of Orange was vital to England's own defence. Now his task, though far from hopeless, was made infinitely more difficult by reason of her prevarications.[54] The hopes of Netherlands unity had been severely damaged; the risks of a deep fracture alarmingly increased.

Orange was in no position to refuse the help of Casimir, though he regarded him with polite contempt and made it plain he was no substitute whatever for Leicester and an English army. He was, of course, well aware that, for Elizabeth, Casimir's task was not to save the Netherlands. He was there to offset the altogether too successful Spanish manœuvres in the south, and the plans of those Walloon nobles who, like Lalaing, the Stadholder of Hainault, inclined to the French and were now engaged in the coquetries preliminary to bringing on the scene Francis, Duke of Anjou, brother of the French King. Physically repulsive and personally despicable he might be, but the Duke could not be ignored. Was this only a French faction – a combination of Huguenots and *politiques* putting their finger into the Netherlands pie? Or was it all done with the connivance of the French King and the Queen Mother? Whichever it was, the prospect was alarming. Having failed to send her own troops in time to contain this new threat, the Queen could hope for little more than that Casimir would temporarily hold the fort. He was a poor thing; a basement bargain. His true cost was only to be reckoned up later.

4 The Loss of the South

THE division of the Netherlands was to mean, in the end, not merely a political frontier dividing Holland from Belgium but a separation and polarisation of economic, social and religious forces. The difference between south and north in Burgundian days had been mainly one between richer and poorer, feudal and less feudal. Gradually the balance was to alter, the pattern to become more complex – in the south, Catholic, bureaucratic, 'obedient'; in the north, Protestant, bourgeois, commercial. A major accelerator of this process was the increasing physical migration from south to north.

In the 1570s these processes had not gone very far. Few of the nobles were clear in their minds which signpost to follow. Should loyalty to the lawful but offending sovereign prevail? Should they follow Orange? Should they turn to France? or to England? It was their knowledge that the situation was so fluid, the defensive strength of the rebels so great, the mass of the noble *politiques* so impressionable, successive Spanish Governors so despairing of success, the ultimate danger to England so great, which influenced some of the Queen's best-informed advisers to favour firm intervention in favour of Orange. By 1578 she had already herself twice decided in favour of such a policy, with even the circuitous Burghley in support. The English role was not peripheral but central. Elizabeth was well aware of this. Yet instead of effective aid and action, she chose to inflict upon the already distracted Netherlands three of the most unattractive adventurers of the age. John Casimir, Elector Palatine-Regent, Anjou and Leicester were directly or indirectly the Queen's choice and responsibility, an economical surrogate, as she thought, for the action for which Orange asked and which she herself had promised. This in itself was bad enough. What was worse was that she chose to insert them into history at the moment when Spain had chosen as its new leader in the Netherlands a man of commanding presence, military genius and subtle intelligence – Alexander Farnese, Prince of Parma.

Meanwhile Don John still lived, and the Queen turned again to what Walsingham called 'the old, useless expedient' of attempted mediation. The following months of 1578 were to see the last chances of effective help for the Netherlands as a whole frittered away. Casimir himself was the first casualty. He was supposed to provide the cavalry strength which the States-General's forces lacked so badly. Duly, if reluctantly, Elizabeth dispatched the necessary £20,000 – ingots packed in barrels like herrings, with a layer of pewter on top to mislead potential malefactors.[1] This *douceur* did not last Casimir long. Soon his troops were raiding the countryside for fodder and food along with the other mercenaries. Casimir's military operations need not detain us. He failed to link up with the States-General army or to give the cavalry support they desperately needed. He repaired, instead, to Ghent, now more than ever the centre of the Protestant fanatics, and joined himself to them, making mischief wherever he went against the Queen who was paying him; worse still, against Orange. The Queen's repeated rebukes finally reached their climax in the autumn of 1578 as she slowly realised the Casimir's pseudo-theocratic antics were a major irritant alienating the Walloon nobility, both Catholic and *politique*, and driving them into the arms of the French.[2] As Professor Stone has said, the achievement of Elizabeth's lieutenant was to thwart the moderating policy of Orange and make the split between Catholics and Calvinists inevitable.[3] Whereupon this ludicrous puppet finally departed, leaving his German troops, without pay or sustenance, to ravage the countryside until they were commanded by Farnese to leave the Netherlands or be exterminated. (This disastrous episode, so prophetic of the later and larger disaster that was to befall Leicester, had a characteristically bizarre conclusion. On the Queen's invitation, Casimir retired to England, where he was feasted and flattered like a returning hero and invested with the Order of the Garter.)

That was the end of Casimir but not of his costs. The loan of over £100,000 which Elizabeth had negotiated through the London banker Horatio Palavicino, a sizeable share of which went on Casimir, continued to bedevil Anglo-Dutch relations for twenty years or more. For many of the Netherlands towns which gave bonds as security for the loan later surrendered to Spain. The burden therefore fell on Holland and Zeeland; but they naturally refused to accept the responsibility for paying either interest or principal. Palavicino, trained in an old Genoese family bank at Antwerp, was not the man to give up his own claim

PLATE I. Cock's view of Antwerp in 1557, showing the strength and completeness of the fortifications

WESTMONASTERII:

DEO EX

R Gaywood.

PLATE II. *The tomb of Sir Francis Vere in Westminster A*

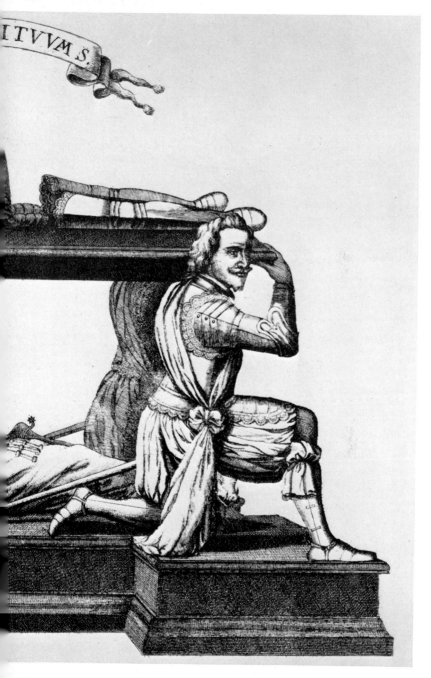

arble and modelled on the tomb of Engelbert of Nassau at Breda)

PLATE III. *Sir Francis Vere*

without a struggle. The wrangles continued into the 1590s. Such were some of the economic consequences of Casimir.

Meanwhile the Queen was already plunged, partly by her own devices, into another and far more serious muddle. Partly as a consequence of Casimir, she now faced a new danger from the pro-French noble faction in the southern Netherlands led by Lalaing, Montigny and Hèze; they wanted to bring in the Duke of Anjou to offset (on the one hand) the risk that Orange might prove too strong for their liking, and (on the other) the certainty that Matthias of Austria would prove too weak. As brother of the French King, he had resources, though it seems that the royal support so feared by contemporaries was not in fact amongst them. Physically, Hercules Francis, the new saviour, was, to say the least, repellent – small, pockmarked and misshapen. As to his character, Motley, in a relatively charitable moment, remarks that history must retain him if only to illustrate the amount of mischief which could be perpetrated by a prince who was 'ferocious without courage, ambitious without talent and bigoted without opinions'.[4] Dangerous, however, he could be, and the Queen now had to face the fact that her failure to give any effective help to Orange had given the Walloon nobility a perfect excuse for an approach to France. Nobody else at this stage was anxious to see anything but the back of Anjou. It is only fair to say that Anjou had a generous endowment of one quality indispensable in a politician: persistence. It is only fair to Elizabeth to add that, regardless of the Netherlands, her problems were multiplying daily. In Ireland and in France rumours spread of anti-English plots, and the possibility of the marriage of Mary, Queen of Scots and Don John was once again in the air. While Burghley retreated again into his balancing calculations, Walsingham did not hesitate to press upon the Queen the evidence that her shifts, prevarications and broken pledges were driving Orange himself into the arms of the French.[5]

All this was intensely irritating to the Queen as she brooded angrily at Greenwich. As usual her wrath fell upon those nearest, if not dearest, to her. Walsingham was curtly instructed to rebuke Davison in the strongest language for dealing 'as an agent for the Prince rather than for Her Majestie . . .'.[6] The memory of his misdemeanours was no doubt kept green against the future. All the same the Queen was deeply anxious, and in June she dispatched

Walsingham and Lord Cobham, a Court favourite and father of the future conspirator,* to the Netherlands on yet another mission. The importance she attached to it was demonstrated by the train of a hundred and twenty advisers, secretaries, aides and servants that accompanied them. It must have been as painful a diplomatic extravagance as any the Queen had yet borne, and one of the most pointless.

The political structure of the party was carefully arranged. Lord Cobham was as far towards Popery and Spain as Walsingham was towards Geneva and the rebels. The equilibrium, nicely calculated by Burghley, was reflected accurately in the instructions to the envoys. First – and how Walsingham must have groaned – came the stale old ritual. 'A good and sure peace between the King of Spain and his subjects' was the object most desirable to the Queen. If this proved impossible, they were to find out what the French were up to. If the French object was to preserve Netherlands independence (how could it be?), they might be given moral support; but if it was to conquer the Low Countries for France, they should consider backing the Spaniards and the States against the French. Finally they might consider – but only as a last resort – what England should do to help. Unpromising as the overtures seemed, the ambassadors were not unduly discouraged. Henry Killigrew, a member of the mission detailed to make a political reconnaissance of the south, came back with an encouraging report.[7] The towns (he wrote) were busy with their New Draperies and other manufactures. They were rich and many were well fortified. The people were generally anti-Spanish and longed for peace. Killigrew discerned amongst them three sorts of opinion. The strongest faction was what he called 'the secret Protestants'. With them were joined the *bons patriots*, most of them 'papists but not fanatical'. These two formed a majority party which broadly favoured toleration. The weakest were 'the passionate papists called Johannists' – 'Pater Noster Jacks' – who would rather have Don John's rule than tolerate heresy. But Killigrew did not think

---

* William, seventh Lord Cobham (d. 1597), was Lord Warden of the Cinque Ports, Lord Lieutenant of Kent, Lord Chamberlain of the Queen's Household and Constable of the Tower, where his son Henry Brooke, eighth Lord Cobham, was to die a prisoner in 1619. The seventh Lord was also familiar with the Tower, where he had been temporarily confined in 1572 on suspicion of being implicated in the plot to marry Mary Stuart to the Duke of Norfolk. The incident does not seem to have lost him the Queen's favour in any degree.

them numerous. 'The gentlemen' were 'for the most part papists.' But again not fanatical. Meanwhile two other Commissioners, Carew and Pelham, visited other fortified towns. Like Davison before them,* they were especially impressed by the strength of Ghent, where the defences had just been renewed,[8] but generally, as they went south, the proportion of papists became larger.[9]

The embassy's first reception by the Prince of Orange was cool. But, as Walsingham later explained to Leicester, this was because – characteristically – he had been given no indication by the English of their business, much less of their powers to do anything to help him. And the Prince was not a man to wear his heart on his sleeve to strangers. Discussion quickly convinced Walsingham that William was in no way inclined to France unless he was driven that way by force. 'The more I deal with him the more suffycyent I fynde him.'[10]

In short, the mission seemed to be going well. They formed the firm opinion that Holland and Zeeland were easily defensible, many towns throughout the country were heavily fortified, and the people were ready to fight indefinitely, 'the quarrel being for libertie'. Then came a remarkable victory in the field, which showed that the defeat at Gembloux had failed to eliminate the States-General army as a fighting force. This return fixture was fought at Rijmenant, a small village not far from Malines, on the first two days of August 1578. Like Gembloux, this battle was also in the open country. The field command of Count Bossu, once Alba's lieutenant, was skilful enough thoroughly to rout the Spanish and loyalist forces under Don John and Farnese.[11] Boussu had the support of a small but vigorous force of Scots and English under Colonel John Norris, of whom much was to be heard later. The Scots 'did greatly shew their wallew and so valyentlye followed and maynteynede the action' that an enemy force of 10,000 foot and 2000 horse 'was repulsed and followed by our nation abowt a myle'. Norris especially won himself 'great credit and honnor'.[12]

Rijmenant showed how precarious the situation of the Spaniards was. It also showed that in open fighting, as distinct from siege warfare, the honours between loyalists and rebels were no more than even. If the English contingent had been anywhere near the size Elizabeth had promised; if Casimir's force had been present

* See p. 60.

and active instead of lying idle, unpaid, without munitions or artillery near Deventer, a hundred miles away; or if the chase of the retreating enemy had been pressed, Rijmenant might have been a decisive victory. But, as after Gembloux, the victors completely failed to follow up and press their advantages, and Rijmenant merely illustrated once again the casual insouciance of sixteenth-century warfare. It proved in particular how the English military contribution, such as it was, was frittered away by utter mismanagement. After the battle the English troops, unpaid and undisciplined, roamed off on private pillaging expeditions, to be killed, to die of disease or simply to desert and disappear.[13]

The consequences of Rijmenant on the morale of the people were serious. If such a victory could end in mere devastation and the spoliation of friend and foe alike, why go on? Even the Prince was not immune from the gathering resentment and discontent.[14]

If the Prince's prestige was now in doubt, the Queen's had fallen to vanishing-point. Once again, at a moment when even Burghley was at one with Leicester in urging effective aid to the rebels and support to Walsingham and Cobham, the Queen turned on the whole lot of them in a towering rage, threatening to hang both Walsingham and Cobham. In Burghley's diplomatic understatement, the Queen was 'very sharp' with them all, ostensibly about money. But it soon became plain there was more to her irascibility than that. Walsingham was appalled to discover that she was intending to resume the marriage proposal with Anjou which had wasted at least four years earlier. Now it was apparent that 'he interteyneth her at this present only to abhuse her, thereby to wyn her the better to disjeast his proceedings heere. I see no remedye but that he is lykly to carrye away thes countreyes.'[15]

Walsingham's fears were soon realised. The 'dear Frog' began his wooing all over again, and the Queen's behaviour and policy took on an air of frenzied improvisation that spread chaos in all directions. Thoroughly alarmed by the news that Anjou had made an agreement with the States-General, she flew into a panic and wrote distractedly to her ambassadors at Antwerp of plans to send ten or twelve thousand men to check the mischiefs being perpetrated by her French suitor. Walsingham, writing 'with a weary hand and a wounded mind', and Wilson, suspended (as he said) 'betwixte hope and feare', were galvanised in mid-August by messages from the Court, now on a royal progress to Norwich, which told of Leicester's appointment to arrange all preparations for raising troops for the Low Countries.[16]

It need hardly be explained that nothing of the kind happened. Wilson, like the rest of the Queen's advisers, was at his wits' end to know how to deal with the stream of contradictory orders with which he was now inundated from the throne. At one and the same time the Queen was throwing the Low Countries into Anjou's lap, alternately cossetting and insulting her 'dear Frog', while coquetting with Don John. '. . . unto whome', cried the distracted Secretary, 'shal wee goe? To our knowen enemyes and to those that are sworne agaynst us for our profession in God's trewthe? Then the lamb shalbee committed to the wolfe and what wyl folowe afterwardes but utter myre and destruction to this lande?'[17] Politics (as Creighton remarked of the French marriage episode) 'never sunk to a lower level of absurdity than in these ridiculous proceedings'.[18]

As William had predicted, the Queen's frivolity now began to have desperately serious repercussions in the Low Countries. About this there was no difference of opinion between Walsingham and Cobham. The uncertainty of her dealings, wrote Walsingham from Antwerp early in September 1578, 'hathe greatly alienated the peoples hartes here, so that . . . they will no longer depende on you'. A week later Cobham reinforced Walsingham's rebuke. The whisperings, the rumours and the deepening suspicion that the Queen had decided to forsake the Netherlands were breeding confusion and desperation. The people and the army were equally discontented and disillusioned by her methods. Even Casimir, his forces still unpaid, was grown 'to a marvelus discontentation'. Cobham repented that he had ever been employed in such negotiations. The Commissioners had spared neither life nor travail to advance Her Majesty's cause. Now he begged Burghley to bring them home. Walsingham echoed his prayer – 'our taryinge now beinge as it were a death to us, for that we are ashamed to look men in the face . . .'.[19] He could only conclude that God had 'closed up Her Majestys hart from seeing and executing that which may be for her safety'.

On the same day Walsingham wrote a separate and special dispatch to the Lord Chancellor. Christopher Hatton was a current intimate favourite – rumour said paramour – of the Queen. Eloquent, plausible, ambitious, Hatton was a *politique* of *politiques*; but his immediate significance was that he was one of the most active promoters of the Anjou marriage plan (and later prosecutor of John Stubbes, the Norfolk Puritan zealot who led the attack on the proposal in the following year). Walsingham did not mince words. 'If it be good', he wrote from Antwerp, 'to have these countries possessed by the Frenche and alienated in good wil from the Crowne of Englande, then you have returned Mr Sommers with a very good dispatche. . . . Surely these people [the Netherlanders] meane no longer to depende upon your uncertainties . . . they shall be forced to have recourse to a most perillous remedie such as may be termed *medecina morbo deterior.*'[20]

In all Elizabeth's strange and tortuous dealings with the Low Countries, few are stranger than these. By her own action or inaction she had driven the States into the arms of the French, the one risk she had always regarded as the major peril to her own safety. Victory at Rijmenant had put her into a strong position to order Casimir and his forces into action against the Spaniards. Yet in the absence of pay, Casimir was more intent on making mischief by encouraging the Calvinist demagogues at Ghent than on making war on the enemy. Don John's forces, also unpaid and now harassed by pestilence, had never been more vulnerable. Now, if ever, the Queen had her chance. Once again she did nothing, and by doing nothing encouraged all the forces which were hostile towards her. Once again it was left to Orange to try and tranquillise the passions of bigotry and ambition now raging at Ghent, where the Calvinists, egged on by the Queen's protégé, Casimir, wrecked Orange's hopes of Netherlands unity by arresting the leading Roman Catholic nobles. These included several formerly ranged against Spain – Hèze, Glymes and Champagny himself ('of the great lewd House of Granvelle' as one of Walsingham's party reminded a correspondent).[21]

In the middle of the confusion, the English mission was suddenly withdrawn. Neither Walsingham nor Cobham had reaped any harvest except of kicks and debts. Three months of negotiation had been totally wasted simply because the Queen would not support them in the work she had sent them to do.[22] They returned, exhausted and disillusioned, understandably wondering whether their royal mistress was entirely sane. 'God send me well to return', wrote Walsingham, 'and I will hereafter take my leave of foreign service.'[23]

And now a dramatic change came over the scene. The ambassadors had only been home a short time when Don John died of the plague which was raging in his army. Like Requesens, he too was exhausted by the incessant anxiety of trying to get money and decisions out of Philip II. For the trials of Elizabeth's advisers and commanders were only exceeded by those suffered by the servants of His Most Christian Majesty of Spain. 'Our life is doled out to us here by moments', Don John had written to the Spanish envoy in Genoa shortly before he died. He too was unpaid and unrewarded; ironically, he believed himself to be helpless before the French threat of invasion. His last letters make derisory any idea that there was anything predetermined about the victory of Spain in the south.[24]

The hero's body, disembowelled and embalmed, was said to have been divided gruesomely into three parts, to be privily and economically[25] transported back to Spain through France in three sacks to be buried in the Escorial. His heart was left at Namur, buried in the church and commemorated by an inscription prepared by his successor, Alexander Farnese. A few days after the funeral rites at Namur, the epigrapher became the new Governor. Handsome, devout, temperate, he was the embodiment of physical bravery in battle. He was also exceedingly intelligent, as patient and sinuous in diplomatic intrigue as he was swift and decisive on the battlefield. For the first time Spain was represented by a leader who was politically a match for Orange and Elizabeth, and their superior as a military leader.

When Don John died, the seventeen provinces were still a 'community'; and in spite of growing tension between the extreme wings of Catholics and Protestants, it was a community still at war, not so much with its lawful sovereign as with 'the Spaniards'.[26] Yet already cracks had appeared in the formal unity of the opposition to Spain. The Walloon troops, who had acquitted themselves a good deal less than creditably at Gembloux, had been sulking resentfully ever since. Now they were drawn together under the leadership of Montigny (a Lalaing). This was the beginning of the so-called Malcontent movement, which was to gather force over the winter months amongst the Walloon provinces. On the other hand, at Ghent, chaos reigned as the Protestant fanatics threatened to hang Champagny and the other Catholic nobles whom they had flung into jail. 'Unhappy', sighed the pious Dr Wilson, 'is the country where the meanest sorte has the greatest swaye, for in a base multitude is never seen good counsel or sound judgement. God help England from any such confused authority.'[27]

It was Farnese's first task to multiply as fruitfully as he could these divisions and anxieties. His way had been made smoother by Casimir's intervention at Ghent, by Anjou's withdrawal from the Low Countries in order to pursue the marriage project in England, and by Elizabeth's refusal to give any support to Orange, whose private fortune had by now disappeared down the bottomless pit of war costs. Without money, his ability either to fight or to compete with Farnese in offering the Walloons any tangible rewards for their support was hopelessly hobbled. So while Burghley continued to write out his lines, piously hoping for the best in the worst of all possible worlds, and the Queen composed excoriating but quite ineffective rebukes to Casimir for his 'evil carriage' at Ghent, the south began to slide into a civil war.

By December Davison in Antwerp was reconciled to the loss of the Walloon provinces. Not only Artois and Hainault but Flanders too were now threatened by total chaos. Walloons were attacking Flemings, Casimir's 'mutynous brood' at Ghent were persecuting the Catholics and being in turn chased by the Spaniards, the States army was disintegrating, the peasants covertly slaughtering the gentry and being 'spoiled and abused' in turn by the mutinous and starving soldiers.[28] Dr Wilson, from a safe distance at Richmond, comforted Davison with the reflection that these were a people 'that can nyther tel how to rewle nor yet can yeelde to be rewled . . . [who] need no adversarie to overthrowe them beinge so moche their owne foes as one wilbe readie to overthrow an other'.[29]

By the winter of 1578–9 the door of success was ajar to Spain, and Farnese was pushing at it hard with all the military and financial means he could muster. At this stage money was a more potent weapon than soldiers. Farnese was not the first to bribe an opponent. The treatment had begun in his predecessor's time, but Don John had had neither the resources nor the energy nor the intelligence to grasp the full promise of the method if systematically applied. One influential convert had nevertheless been made – the Seigneur la Motte, Governor of Gravelines, not quite a gentleman but a good professional soldier, cheap at three hundred florins a month. A small gain perhaps, but it showed what could be done and was increasingly to be done. La Motte was followed by a small procession of ecclesiastics, all ready to forget their grievances against Spain at the thought of a mitre. Of these, the Abbot of St Vaast, Jean Sarrasin, deft, accomplished and eloquent, was the most useful. After that the trickle became a flood. The resistance of the south – not only of the Walloon provinces – already weakened by migration, by quarrels and a spreading pessimism, collapsed under the weight of bribery. The French envoy, des Pruneaux, let Catherine de Medici into the secret of success. 'The ducats of Spain, Madam,' he wrote, 'are trotting about in such fashion that they have vanquished a great quantity of courage. Your Majesty must employ more money if you wish to advance one step.'[30]

Early in 1579 Farnese, through La Motte, was haranguing and bribing the Walloon nobles, especially the House of Croy, back to loyalty. The very terms of the Arras treaty, by which the Spanish troops were bustled out of the Netherlands, released valuable funds for political purposes. Honey caught more flies than vinegar. Montigny, already head of the Malcontent troops, was purchased for 200,000 guilders in April. His brother Lalaing went over a little later. Melun, Viscount of Ghent,* was followed by Havrech, Egmont, Hèze and Capres. Aerschot made his peace later. Rennenberg, Stadholder of Groningen, also a Lalaing and so far a loyal supporter of Orange, held out until 1580, when he too capitulated, taking Groningen with him. By that time the Netherlands had been divided into two Unions. The Union of Utrecht, formed in January 1579, had Holland and Zeeland as its base, but it also still included Ghent, Antwerp, Breda and non-Walloon Flanders. It might, as the States of Hainault alleged, be a 'heretical' union. But it was not as yet merely a northern one. Utrecht in turn hastened the formal creation of a Catholic union, the Union of Arras, in May.[31] But again, if it was Catholic, it was not (in the modern sense) 'Belgian', for it was limited to Wallonia. Drawing the final lines of division between north and south was to be military, not political, work.[32]

By mid-summer there were few nobles left on the side of the States. As one of Davison's correspondents had put it: 'The war which is about to begin will be a war for religion; the cloak of which the malcontent lords will adopt in order the better to satisfy their ambition, hatred and avarice, and get rid of the Prince of Orange, to whom they bear deadly ill-will.'[33] This was an

* Later Marquis of Richebourg and Roubaix. Killed at Antwerp, 1585.

overstatement. Many of the nobles were now more vulnerable to bribery, quite simply because inflation was continuously eroding the real value of their incomes from land. Others still wanted to go back to the Pacification of Ghent and were genuinely alarmed by the wild fanaticism of the Ghent Calvinists, egged on as they were by Elizabeth's protégé, Casimir. If Orange could have held out a fraction of the material *douceurs* offered by Farnese, history might have been very different. As it was, support for his policies disappeared only when it became clear that he had been deserted by Elizabeth.* Farnese himself had no illusions about his own difficulties. Every letter from Farnese to Philip II at this stage, and indeed for most of the next decade, lamented the poverty to which he was reduced by the parsimony and ignorance at Madrid, and the magnitude of the military and political tasks which faced him.[34] His intransigeant insistence, even to Philip, on preserving the unity of his military and political command grew not least from his conviction that without supreme power, he would find the Walloon nobility in turn deserting him again for Orange.

Again, if Elizabeth had not destroyed Orange's confidence, things might have turned out very differently. The provinces comprehended within the Union of Utrecht showed remarkable powers of resilience. Reluctantly – but with England out of the running there seemed no alternative – the Duke of Anjou had to be brought back to succeed as sovereign. Davison, back in Antwerp, had done his best to alert the Council to the perils Anjou posed for England as the potential 'defender of Netherlands liberties' and royal suitor – '. . . a stranger, a borne ennemy, in manners, religion, and in nature discrepant from us' – to say nothing of his being a prime agent of the national enemy, France.[35] But neither his pleadings nor those of Leicester or Walsingham had any effect – until after Elizabeth put the ring on Anjou's finger in November 1581. Then she came back to her senses with a start. All her old anti-French phobias were aroused. In a frenzy she switched back to the policies urged on her for years by Walsingham, though retaining a curious, nostalgic *schwärmerei* for her 'Frog', perhaps of the kind princes reserved for court jesters, dwarfs or buffoons. Parma watched the Queen's goings-on with amused contempt. 'The

---

* See p. 133 for a comparison with the events of 1640–1 and the critical importance attached by the then Stadholder to a Stuart marriage for the prestige of his 'dynasty'.

marriage of that Queen', he wrote to the Spanish Ambassador in London, 'seems to me like the weaving of Penelope, undoing every night what was done the day before and then reweaving it anew the next, advancing in these negotiations neither more nor less than has been done and undone countless times without reaching a conclusion one way or the other. And in this way the years will pass her by, so that there will be very little to desire in her. However, your Lordship will know better than I to what ends this is done. . . .'[36]

In his new Netherlands dignity, Hercules Francis was to be 'helped' – watched, that is, for rightly he was trusted by nobody – by a Council of State. Even so, his reign was short and disastrous, ending in violence, mutiny and humiliation. The provinces over which he presided had now all abjured the rule of Philip. The 'Placard of Diffidation' (July 1581) was the work not of a Hollander or a Zeelander but of a Brabanter, Jan van Asseliers, brother-in-law of William's adviser, van Wesembeeck, and a high official of the Antwerp government and of the States-General. Its reasoning was medieval and feudal, rather than Calvinist. It aligned itself with the arguments of William of Orange's *Apology* of the same year, and it demonstrated that the revolt was not yet by any means severed from the past or from its 'Burgundian' aim of unity.[37]

This, and the slow progress of Farnese, shows how disastrously casual were the factors which ultimately divided the Netherlands. Farnese's difficulties were obvious and formidable. Until 1582 he was hampered by the terms of the Peace of Arras which had insisted that the Spanish troops leave the Netherlands, and by Philip's preoccupations with Portugal, where Alba had recovered his health and spirits sufficiently to invade, sack and pillage, crushing any resistance with cruelties as atrocious as anything he had committed in the Netherlands. Throughout 1580 and 1581 Parma set himself two successive tasks. The first was to win popular confidence: this he achieved by behaving with studied moderation. That done, he set himself to get his Spaniards back, explaining repeatedly to the Walloon States that without them it was quite impossible for him to conquer the enemy.[38] When Count Lalaing proved recalcitrant, Farnese reduced him through the good offices of the Countess, a close friend. (Venetian Ambassadors to the Low Countries more than once noted the power exercised by the noblewomen over their husbands.) In January 1582 the work was going ahead, though again at inordinate expense in bribes. Lalaing, Richebourg (formerly Viscount Ghent), Montigny, the Abbot of St Vaast and Count Hennin (Bossu's son, now won over by the enticing office of President of the Council of Finance) spread seductive propaganda in Artois. It only remained to rally the Duke of Aerschot. By February the States of the Walloon provinces declared unanimously in favour of the return of the Spanish troops.[39] It had been achieved by the help 'of most discreet persons who had been strategically placed in all the cities to prepare for the decision'. The secret had been so well guarded that any opponents were powerless and taken hopelessly by surprise.

In one respect Farnese's problem was the same as Alba's. Farnese's strategy against the rebels was interrupted at crucial points by the demands of Spanish strategy elsewhere in Europe. In 1581 he was compelled to turn south to face the threat of a French invasion. And except in the Walloon provinces, where everything except Cambrai was overrun by 1579, progress against those fortified towns whose strength had so impressed Carew* was disappointing and frustrating. Before the Spanish troops returned, only one or two towns north of the Walloon area had been taken – Louvain, Gravelines, Groningen and some neighbouring towns, and of course Maastricht. This was the phase of 'consolidation' amongst the anti-Spanish forces in the towns and cities of Brabant and Flanders, the time of a new 'Third Estate' (as one historian has called it).[40] Far from supporting the idea that Flanders and Brabant were indefensible, the three years that followed the Peace of Arras suggested that they were – for all the weakness and mistakes of their defenders – a tough nut to crack. Gravelines and Groningen were betrayed for money or position.[41] Maastricht, the gateway from the Netherlands into Germany, was only taken in 1579 after four months of mining and counter-mining, repeated assaults and counter-assaults. For months Orange had urged upon the States the vital importance of strengthening its defences: all in vain; parochialism, the blessing and the curse of the Netherlands, had doggedly defeated his efforts. But its stubborn defence once again revealed the inherent strength of the south.

Farnese now turned his attention to a group of towns all lying in a narrow circle and strung together along the Scheldt and its

* See p. 67.

tributary the Senne. Learning from his experience at Maastricht, where he had isolated the city by throwing two bridges across the Maas, one above and one below, Farnese now repeated the experiment, but in multiples. Ghent, Dendermonde, Mechlin, Brussels and last but greatest, Antwerp, were to be isolated, and then reduced by famine. Here the great river, so far from being a bulwark of the northerners' defence, was a positive hinrance. Nor did the attackers have to wait for starvation to do their work. Treachery, bribery and bigotry did more than gunpowder or military valour to bring down the walls and bastions, bridge the moats and mine the foundations of the cities. Dendermonde surrendered without a fight. So did Vilvoorde, and its fall cut off the waterway between Brussels and Antwerp. Ghent – 'energetic, opulent, powerful, passionate, unruly Ghent'[42] – the second city of the Netherlands, had for years been in the hands of the Calvinist fanatics. More than once it had nearly been betrayed by the Calvinists to Farnese. Finally it was surrendered, though its moats and bulwarks, ravelins and counterscarps, constructed over the years at enormous expense and only recently renewed, were still intact and it had bread and meat and powder and shot in plenty. But half its working population had fled and the morale of the remainder was too low to sustain a struggle that seemed to have lost its point.[43] Brussels and Mechlin followed. Bruges was betrayed by Aerschot's heir, Prince Chimay, who had recently declared his loyalty to Orange and the States. To the north, Orange's brother-in-law van den Bergh betrayed Zutfen, as Rennenberg had betrayed Groningen. At Nijmegen the Catholic citizens threw out the States garrison and handed the town over to Farnese. Now only Antwerp, Ostend and Sluys remained.

While Farnese prepared his *coup de grâce* for Antwerp, the rebels suffered their worst loss. They had survived with equanimity the death in June 1584 of the *Défenseur de la Liberté Belgique*, the Duke of Anjou. Not many of Orange's colleagues shared his slender hope that the Netherlands' salvation lay in the overlordship of Elizabeth's 'sweet Frog'. But in July William himself, *Pater Patriae*, was assassinated in his house, the Prinsenhof, at Delft. 'As long as he lived, he was the guiding star of a whole brave nation, and when he died the little children cried in the streets.' The concluding words of Motley's epic were not merely a rhetorical tribute to the Prince or to Motley's sensitive ear for a

D

cadence. They came literally from a contemporary official report to the Magistracy of Brussels by the Recorder of the States.[44]

It had nevertheless to be admitted that in the year or more before the assassination William's prestige had slumped heavily. He seemed to many to carry the kiss not of life but of death. Was he not (they muttered) the symbol of defeat, bankruptcy and demands for taxes on a scale threatening to equal those of Spain herself? Even in his own Holland and Zeeland the whisperings multiplied. William remained outwardly unmoved – wise, unflappable, fundamentally optimistic as ever. But his treatment by Elizabeth and by his fellow nobles had left scars. They were plainly visible in his last *Apology*, which was as much an attack on the Malcontent nobles as on Philip himself. In a long stretch of sustained invective they were lashed as faithless, time-serving, corrupt, incapable of loyalty to cause or person, too stupid even to see where their own best interests lay. How could he fail to be indignant at the conduct of those members of noble houses whose fathers he had loved and honoured? 'They serve the Duke of Alba and the Grand Commander like scullions. They make war on me to the knife. Then they treat with me, they reconcile themselves with me, they are sworn enemies of the Spaniards. Don John arrives and they follow after him: they intrigue for my ruin. Don John fails in his enterprises upon the Antwerp citadel; they quit him incontinently and call upon me. No sooner do I come than, against their oath and without telling either the States or me, they call upon the Archduke Matthias. Are the waves of the sea more inconstant – is Euripus* more uncertain than the councils of such men?'[45]

The charges were not unjust. Most of the English observers in the Netherlands in these years said much the same at one time or another. An observant Spaniard[46] later castigated the majority, including Aerschot, Havrech, Aremberg, Berlaymont, Bossu, Ligne, Egmont and Hoogstraten, as weak and faithless, potentially as unreliable towards Spain as William had judged them to be towards himself. But William was the one man who had the indisputable right to lay the charges. If (as his enemies alleged) he had been moved originally by personal ambition, he had certainly purged himself of it. He had bankrupted himself and his family in

---

* The highly dangerous narrow straits that separate Chalcis on Euboea from the mainland.

the cause. He had sacrificed one of the largest fortunes in Europe. He had repeatedly risked, and finally lost, his life. His unique qualities shine through the interviews with him recorded by English agents of all shades of opinion. Even the Queen could not conceal or withhold her admiration. She merely withheld the money, the troops and the means by which he might have consolidated that leadership to which she paid repeated but insubstantial tribute.

Like his successors, Oldenbarneveldt and Maurice, William was neither pro-French nor pro-English: he was pro-Netherlands. It has been argued that William gambled on the constancy of French policy and paid the price. Perhaps; but why? Because Queen Elizabeth hankered after a Spanish alliance as a counterpoise to France and tortured herself – though only intermittently – with nightmares of a gallicised Netherlands. The unfathomably devious diplomatic shiftings and shufflings to which this theory gave rise made it impossible for William to look for help anywhere but in France. It was difficult for others to deny William the right to Anjou as his unwelcome prize when the Queen of England herself was still lamenting (February 1582) that she would give a million pounds that 'her dear Frog should again be swimming in the Thames and not in the marshes of the Low Countries'.[47]

The effect of William's martyrdom – for that was what it seemed to be – was electrifying. Far from deepening the mood of critical despair, it revitalised the Utrecht Union by a wave of sheer anger. At once William's son, young Prince Maurice, still completing his studies at the new University of Leyden, was elected head of a Council of State, a lineal constitutional descendant of the body set up to supervise Anjou. Threatened and shrinking the Union might be, but the new Council still contained representatives from Flanders, Brabant, Mechlin and Friesland as well as from Holland and Zeeland. Acutely aware of the problems they faced, they set to work resolutely and methodically so that, for the time being, the provinces they represented were not seduced by Farnese's bribery like their Walloon neighbours. It was at once agreed that there was to be no truck with Spain; anybody bringing letters or messages to private persons should be hanged forthwith. That sounded the note of resolution observed by William Herle, the Queen's agent present at the scene. At Dordrecht he had a characteristic visitation from the local regents. They came 'not as men condoling their estate or craving courage to be instilled into them – though wanting now a head – but irritated above measure to be revenged and to defend all their heads, so apparently sought for by the King of Spain, in murdering their head, the Prince of Orange'. Throughout the country, the general reaction was the same. There was 'no dismay at all, either of the people or the magistrates' but rather 'a great resolution of courage and hatred engraved in them, to revenge the foulness of the fact committed on the person of the Prince by the tyrant of Spain, and to defend their liberties advisedly against him and his adherents by all means that God has given them, to the uttermost portion of their substance, and the last drop of their blood'.[48]

The new vitality could not of itself save Antwerp, whose capture by Farnese was the heaviest single blow to the rebels since the fall of Maastricht. There is no need to repeat the story of the siege, extraordinary as it is. It has been told many times.[49] It is enough to say that William had been convinced before his death that Antwerp, the hinge of the Netherlands, was perfectly defensible. Antwerp lay on the edge of the Netherlands water area. William's plan therefore was to open the major dykes and flood the land surrounding the city north of the river Scheldt. The approaches from the sea to the city would then no longer be limited to the relatively narrow and vulnerable river channel of the Scheldt itself, but would be broadened out enormously, until the city could be supplied from the sea via the Zeeland estuary.

The siege showed that his plan was perfectly correct and practicable. It was simply never executed. In the confusion that followed his death, no leader emerged to exercise effective military and political control of the city. Marnix St Aldegonde, whom William had sent there to prepare for the expected siege, had neither the temperament, experience nor authority to impose discipline or unity on the many conflicting interests within the city. So, while Farnese, with a relatively small attacking force, was steadily isolating Antwerp from Ghent, the city fathers were quarrelling about the best ways of stopping him. Petty commanders wrangled incessantly among themselves. The butchers' guild successfully postponed the flooding of pastures so valuable to their meat trade until it was too late. Parma captured the vital dykes, cutting Antwerp off from its potential saviours in Zeeland. Hohenlo, the States commander, allowed his troops to go off looting instead of attending to their job of capturing Farnese's central supply base at 's Hertogenbosch. Zutfen seemed more important to defend than Antwerp.

By 15 February 1585 Farnese was ready to implement his grand plan and cut off Antwerp from the sea by a great new bridge. Even when it was built, Farnese's task was not done. His bridge was breached by an exploding fireship built by Gianibelli, an Italian inventor from Mantua who lived in Antwerp; but the signal conveying the news of its success was never given, and the planned infantry assault that was to follow never materialised. A little later it seemed certain that the great Kouwensteyn dyke, key to the flooding, had been recaptured from the Spaniards. Indeed a signal victory was reported to Antwerp. Alas! it was only too characteristic of the confusion in which the whole operation was shrouded that the news proved quite untrue. On 17 August St Aldegonde capitulated. Ten days later Farnese entered the city with a contingent of the great Walloon nobles headed by the Duke of Aerschot. Soon after, Champagny was appointed Governor. But we must now turn back to see what Elizabeth and her advisers had been concerting in face of the new threat from Farnese.

Even though Elizabeth 'had no enthusiasm for a cause'[50] and had only 'that capacity for consistency which consisted in always being inconsistent',[51] the threat to Antwerp undoubtedly filled her with anxiety. For several years, in spite of her almost pathological fear of France, she had played with the idea of a Franco-English condominium in the Netherlands. Then the disturbing progress of the Franco-Dutch negotiations in 1584 had given her pause for thought. From the start of the rebellion there had been a French faction anxious to get control of the strategically placed island of Walcheren. Now the argument sharpened between the alleged Francophiles in Holland and Zeeland, represented by St Aldegonde and Johan van Oldenbarneveldt, and the supposed Anglophiles, still faithfully led by Paul Buys and Adolf van Meetkerke of Bruges. William's death stimulated Buys into action against what seemed to be the real threat of a Franco-Dutch treaty with Henry III as sovereign of the Netherlands. This was too much for Buys, 'having seen', as he said, 'the scope of that Court'.[52]

Once again, in England, Burghley was piously working over all the old threadbare possibilities of peace between Philip and his rebel subjects. Then in December 1584, thoroughly alarmed by the death of William, Farnese's military progress and the rumours of French political ambitions, Elizabeth decided to send William Davison back on another exploratory mission. His instructions bore all the marks of Burghley's confused caution: his promises of 'all possible assistance' and an inquiry to ascertain 'the proper means of making that assistance most useful' must have reminded the Dutch Council of State all too dismally of the Queen's earlier undertakings. Once more Davison was driven almost distraught with another instalment of unintelligible instructions from Burghley. Once more Walsingham, sceptical and clear-headed, remembering all too vividly the humiliating frustrations of his own recent mission, believed that it was all a waste of time, a pantomime which all the Queen's enemies saw through like glass. Worst of all, she would 'neither help those poor countries nor yet suffer others to do it'.53

In London, however, others were busy spinning out their private ambitions and the public benefits that were supposed to follow from them. The Earl of Leicester was beginning to smell power and powder again. By March 1585 Walsingham was in earnest conference with the Dutch agent in London, Joachim Ortel. Ortel was a London Dutchman, closely bound up with the élite of deacons and elders of the Dutch Church at Austin Friars – Utenhove, Ortelius, van Meteren and Daniel Rogers's family. In an opening skirmish even Walsingham, prodded no doubt by Elizabeth or Burghley, attacked the Dutch for becoming so deeply entangled with France. Ortel, a highly intelligent and capable diplomat, was ready for the attack. He came back with an equally sharp riposte. What had been transacted by the Dutch with France 'was not done except with the express approbation and full foreknowledge of Her Majesty, so far back as the lifetime of His Excellency [the Prince of Orange] of high and laudable memory . . .'.54

Walsingham did not try to argue. He knew only too well how justified Ortel's charge was. From this moment on, the exchanges became unusually cordial. Even the Queen went out of her way to pay the closest attention to Ortel, whom she now treated with a warmth that had been vouchsafed to none of his predecessors. It was unnecessary, she assured him, for her to repeat over again the sentiments of sympathy she had so often expressed to the States. There would be no back-door discussions. She did not want power over the Netherlands; only the preservation of their liberties. And much more in the same vein.[55] This was all splendid. Unfortunately nothing was done. Secretaries and Ambassadors talked on and on, while Farnese's preparations against Antwerp were steadily coming to fruition. Hollanders and Zeelanders wrangled between themselves over the terms of the proposed treaty with England. For the assistance to the Netherlands was not an outright gift. Like lease–lend in 1940, it was essentially a tough pawnbroking exercise, and it was the Zeelanders' most valuable port, Flushing, which was to be their principal pledge.[56] Neither Burghley nor the Queen needed any encouragement to postpone action, but if it were needed it came in the shape of an optimistic dispatch from Gilpin, former Secretary of the Merchant Adventurers in the Netherlands. St Aldegonde, said Gilpin, hoped to clear a passage all the way up to Antwerp, thus frustrating Farnese's hopes of spoiling the city and fomenting mutiny amongst the Spanish troops once more. Farnese, he assured Walsingham comfortingly, was short of money and faced with damaging quarrels amongst the Walloon Malcontent nobility.[57]

The letter could not have been worse timed. Burghley at once told Ortel that the Queen, who had been on the point of ordering troops to Antwerp, would now await the outcome of St Aldegonde's attack on the Kouwensteyn dyke before sending troops. There was no need for any unseemly haste. Gilpin's 'simple, hopeful letter' had, as Ortel wrote bitterly to Walsingham, overthrown everything.'[58] The full force of his judgement was not to be apparent until more than three months later. Meanwhile a strong Dutch mission, led by Oldenbarneveldt, arrived in early July and the talks began in earnest. It was 20 August 1585 (N.S.) before the Treaty of Nonsuch was finally signed. By its terms the Queen took the Low Countries under her protection and promised immediate help.[59] A week earlier she had spoken to the Dutch deputies, who petitioned her urgently for the relief of Antwerp. Already, she assured them, two thousand men under General Norris had crossed or (she corrected herself) were crossing every day by companies. She would hasten the rest to the utmost.[60] In fact none had arrived at either Ostend or Sluys, and the six hundred who had reached Zeeland were totally unprepared to do battle. No more arrived until after Antwerp had officially surrendered on 17 August.[61]

Historians (foreign ones anyway), ancient and modern, have combined to criticise the Queen for these delays. Whatever their disagreements on other matters, Geyl and Motley are at one over this. If the English troops had reached Antwerp in time, Motley wrote, 'it is almost a certainty that Antwerp would have been relieved and the whole of Flanders and Brabant permanently annexed to the independent commonwealth, which would thus have assumed at once most imposing proportions'.[62]

The Queen, wrote Geyl, 'bore a heavy responsibility. Had she, in anticipation of a treaty, sent over a couple of thousand men, Parma, who had barely sufficient troops, would certainly not have been able to make good the losses he suffered.'[63] This is not merely the retrospective view of a Dutch historian. It was shared by many contemporaries, English as well as Dutch. Jacques Rossell,* commissary and intelligence agent at Antwerp, wrote in bitter disillusionment from the Netherlands to Walsingham: 'For my part I am convinced that all this business of help and the fleet and all our enterprises have been mere stratagems. Also, I have never been able to understand how such practices could have been employed with the knowledge of Her Majestie and yourself, *for I know this city could have been relieved*.'[64] John Norris himself said much the same. For months he had been in the Netherlands expecting troops by the thousand. They had arrived by the dozen. Norris, son of the Queen's 'own black crow',† was blunt and outspoken. The surrender of Antwerp, he wrote to the Privy Council, 'gave these people [the Netherlanders] occasion to doubt that Her Majestie had refused them all succour'.[65]

Burghley shared the blame with his mistress. William Herle,[66] an ingenious intriguer employed by Burghley as a spy, and now busy playing off Walsingham against Burghley, wrote ambiguously to the Lord Treasurer as soon as he heard the news of the surrender 'that the rage of men was so great against your Lordship as it exceeded both measure and modesty'. He added helpfully that the disaster was blamed on Burghley's dilatory policy, his doubts and hesitations. England had become, men said, a *regnum Cecilianum*.

* Rossell described himself as a former muster-master in the service of the Prince of Orange and the States. He tried hard to enter the Queen's service first as a serving officer, later as a financial expert, but with what result is not clear.

† Lady Norris, wife of Lord Norris of Rycot, was daughter of Lord Williams of Thame, Keeper of the Tower during Elizabeth's imprisonment. Her loyalty and affection were not forgotten when Elizabeth became Queen.

The Queen and her Council were ruled by him. And so on. There was no doubt some deliberate mischief-making here. Nevertheless it was true that Burghley had on at least four occasions backed down from action on behalf of the Netherlands after giving it his support. He had personally helped to delay the dispatch of help for Antwerp.[67]

The Queen herself, usually so unrepentant under criticism, for once seems to have been shocked into a mood of anxiety and even apology.[68] The degree of her responsibility for the collapse of Antwerp cannot be gauged: it can only be guessed. It is certainly possible that extra troops might have saved the day. Farnese's view of his success, with his troops dressed in rags and tatters, comes out in a plea for help written to Philip immediately afterwards. 'God', he wrote, 'will soon be weary of working miracles for us.' It was victory, but victory by the skin of his teeth. Everything had in the end hinged on the quality of the military command. The local Antwerp command under St Aldegonde was certainly in a hopeless state of confusion. It could well have squandered any more resources given to it. On the other hand, if help had been made contingent upon Norris being given full powers of command, he might well have saved the city. His qualities as a commander were soon to be revealed, and they were not negligible. Second of the six soldier sons of Lord Norris, the famous 'chickens of Mars', he was certainly the ablest English commander in the Netherlands so far.

These are hypotheses. The facts now had to be faced. Farnese was at the height of his powers and the zenith of his career. He had virtually completed the conquest of the southern Netherlands; he had robbed the rebels of Antwerp, their strongest supply point, the richest and one of the largest and most splendid cities of Europe. This symbol of Netherlands resistance to Spain was now to become a major bastion in the strategy of the south against the north. Farnese had emerged as the creator of a Roman Catholic state, obedient to Spain, ancestor of modern Belgium. By contrast England's prospects were daunting. For even as Antwerp tottered to its fall, the Queen had signed a treaty with the rebels which it was now too late to reconsider. By its terms the sovereign who, of all her reigning contemporaries, had achieved a reputation for prudence, even parsimony, ironically found herself bound to provide help for her allies on a scale she could not control and for a length of time no one could foresee. Perhaps it was this, as much as her conscience over Antwerp, which left her so sorely troubled.

5 The North Preserved

THE Treaty of Nonsuch of 1585 committed Elizabeth to maintain a sizeable English Army in the Netherlands. Five thousand foot and a thousand horse were to serve at the Queen's expense – temporarily. Article 2 of the Treaty hastened to make it clear that there was to be no loose generosity and that all the Queen's outlay would be repaid within five years of the signing of a peace. As on many later occasions of a similar kind, it was optimistically supposed the war would be a short one. By way of security for the cost incurred, the strategically vital ports of Flushing and The Brill were to remain in English hands and be garrisoned at the Queen's expense. What the Queen would not do was to accept the sovereignty of the rebel provinces.[1]

Three months later, in November, she felt moved to issue a declaration to the world justifying her final departure from ten years of attempted benevolent neutrality.[2] In versions published simultaneously in English, Dutch, French and Italian, she declared her unshakeable devotion to the ancient Burgundian alliance, while denouncing Spanish atrocities committed not only against Protestant subjects but against Catholics too. Conveniently oblivious of her earlier refusal to lift a finger to help Egmont, she referred particularly to him who, of all the nobility maltreated by the King, had deserved best of Spain and been most cruelly victimised as a loyal subject and a Catholic. The Netherlands themselves had been laid waste, but it was not only the Netherlands against which Philip had offended. She herself and her realm had been the target for conspiracies in England, Ireland and Scotland. Her aims were threefold: a general peace; the recognition of religious freedom and the restoration of the ancient liberties of the Netherlands; and security for England, which could only enjoy tranquillity when the Low Countries were tranquil. It might have been a declaration by Orange himself, for certainly all the major objectives for which he had striven were now conceded by the Queen. It showed at any rate that he had not lived or died in vain. Philip made immediate and predictable reply, ordering all English as well as Netherlands ships in Spanish ports to be seized forthwith, together with persons and property. War was declared. The only question was what form it was to take. Planning began almost at once.

For the Queen there were two questions to be answered: who was to manage the Netherlands enterprise and what were to be his instructions? For a decade or more Robert Dudley, Earl of Leicester, Elizabeth's 'Sweet Robin', had set his cap at the Netherlands. His affair with the Queen had been long, passionate, stormy and dubious. Evidently he possessed a certain animal magnetism which she found irresistible. His marital affairs, including as they did the unsolved mystery of Amy Robsart's death, a bigamous marriage to Lady Essex, and recurrent rumours of his implication in poisonings, had not increased his popularity with Queen or people. Handsome in youth, he was now (as he himself engagingly remarked) high-coloured and red-faced. Like his grandfather and father, he was cruel, rapacious for money and greedy for power. Unlike them, he combined a genuine love of the drama and of poetry – his own letters are lively, spontaneous and entertaining – with a willingness to assume the leadership of the Puritan faction in high politics. Any political mount was better than none. His occupation of the office of High Steward of the University of Cambridge did nothing to clear him of the charge that he was also a fundamentally stupid man. Worst of all, this *arriviste*, miniature Borgia in pasticcio, could not bear to have his wisdom questioned. Any critic, however old and loyal a friend, was automatically condemned to be his sworn enemy.

Close as he was to the Queen, avid as was his desire to be the chosen vessel, it was far from a foregone conclusion as late as September that he would lead the expeditionary force to the Low Countries. Walsingham himself thought Elizabeth was not disposed to use Leicester's services. The lot of governor, he supposed, would light on Lord Grey. Arthur, fourteenth Lord Grey de Wilton, had much to recommend him. He came of an ancient line, he was the close friend of Burghley and he had proved a tough and determined Lord Deputy of Ireland. Unfortunately he suffered from one irremediable weakness, which the Queen could not disregard or forgive. He had spent his whole life in the valley of the shadow of debt, and his recent gallant service in Ireland had proved the last financial straw. 'I would to God', wrote Walsingham, 'the ability of his purse were answerable to his sufficiency otherwise.'[3]

There were other possibilities: Roger, second Lord North, for example, who had already shown himself a tactful and successful diplomatist in difficult situations in France. His intelligence and fortitude were to be tested many times in the next few years. Leicester was to think of him as a possible successor two years later. So did Peregrine Bertie, Lord Willoughby, who was to succeed Leicester. Willoughby was a devoted follower of Leicester, brave, choleric and hot-tempered, despising the art of words and diplomacy:

> The brave Lord Willoughby
> Of courage fierce and fell
> Who would not give one inch of way
> For all the devils in Hell.

'I ambitiously affect not high titles', he wrote to Leicester, 'but round dealing, desiring rather to be a private lance with indifferent reputation than a colonel general spotted or defamed with wants.'[4] Willoughby was brave, at heart oddly diffident, and no fool; but in 1585 he was certainly not an obvious choice. For one thing, like Lord Grey, he was impoverished and his estates were mortgaged up to the hilt. Nor unfortunately was Sir Philip Sidney. Orange himself had thought highly of Sidney – 'one of the ripest and greatest counsellors of state . . . that hold in Europe'.[5] Sidney was almost as widely known and esteemed in the Low Countries as in England. But he was misliked by the Queen, traduced by Burghley, and in any case could hardly be promoted over the head of his uncle, Leicester.

That left only one formidable candidate, and it is not clear that he was even seriously considered. Thomas Sackville, Lord Buckhurst, later first Earl of Dorset, author of *Gorboduc*, poet, dramatist, model for Edmund Spenser, was one of the most talented and elegant ornaments of Elizabeth's Court. He was also a prudent, sagacious man (later to be Chancellor of Oxford University), a persuasive orator and skilled negotiator who was to succeed Burghley as Lord Treasurer.[6] At Knole he created the great house which was to be the home of a rich cultural tradition: its reflections have lingered down to our own day.[7] A dutiful public servant, Buckhurst was to negotiate a sensible if unheroic pathway between the vicious jealousies, factions and rivalries of Elizabeth's Court, emerging nearly (though not quite) unscathed. Time and again he was employed as a successful trouble-shooter, landing in prison only once.

'Sackville's sonnets sweetly saust' were not his only achievement. Only a year later he was to be saddled with the unenviable task of sorting out the muddle in Anglo-Netherlands relations created by Leicester. Why not earlier? It probably came back to Walsingham's proposition: no one but Leicester could command the combination of private fortune and social prestige which the Queen thought to be necessary in the man who was to combine the political and military leadership in the Low Countries, to succeed to the Archduke of Austria and the Duke of Anjou. If the two offices were to continue as one, a great lord was demanded, in this case one who could dig deeply into his own pocket and for that reason, if no other, could command the support of the Queen. So the job went to Leicester. No one except Buckhurst seems to have considered (what would undoubtedly have been a better solution) dividing the purely military command from the political governorship. If this had been done there would have been by this time no lack of able officers to direct military affairs – John Norris for example, to whose skill as commander the Netherlands were to owe an incalculable debt. There was Sir William Pelham: true, his temper was as threadbare as his finances, but he had seen thirty-five years of hard service in France and Ireland, which was to be rewarded by his appointment as Marshal of the army in the Netherlands. But in the tangled confusion of private and public interests that characterised the Elizabethan scene, a division of civil and military affairs was too sophisticated a solution to command any attention. So, although his military experience (as Master of the Ordnance in Picardy) was now thirty years old and quite inadequate to qualify him for the post of military leader, Leicester, 'Sweet Robin', became – inevitably – Governor-General. It was to prove – even against stiff competition from a long line of unsuccessful English commanders of overseas expeditionary forces before and since – one of the most disastrous appointments of its kind ever made. Fortunately, and after a long and squalid haggle, it was flanked by some sensible secondary appointments. Sidney, Leicester's nephew and Walsingham's son-in-law, after being nearly blackballed completely, was made commander of Flushing; the Burghley faction was kept quiet by the installation of Burghley's son, Thomas Cecil, as commander of The Brill. John Norris and his brother Edward were already in battle on the Betuwe.* They were joined by a dozen or more

* The long stretch of land between the Rhine and the Waal.

excellent commanders – the Veres, Morgans, Roger Williams, Robert Sidney, Thomas Wilford, William Russell, Lord Willoughby and many others.

It was a formidable company that disembarked at Flushing just before Christmas 1585. Leicester's fifty ships carried 'the flower and chief gallants of England'.[8] Compared with Farnese, the new governor himself might not be overburdened with military experience or brains, but nobody could doubt the fighting spirit and gallantry of his officers and troops. One of Leicester's veterans voiced their stout, uncomplicated Protestant patriotism succinctly. He was Thomas Wilford. 'This war doth defend England . . . the fire is kindled; whosoever suffers it to go out, it will grow dangerous. . . . The whole state of religion is in question. . . . The freehold of England will be worth but little if this action quail and therefore I wish no subject to spare his purse towards it.'[9] Much of the spirit was to be squandered, unfortunately, on the violent internal quarrels which broke out immediately amongst Leicester's officers or between them and their Dutch allies.

But Christmas 1585 seemed to take history back a decade to the old Anglo-Dutch euphoria of 1572. Leicester's party were astonished and delighted by the wealth and goodwill they found everywhere. Richard Cavendish tried to ignite Burghley's damp and cautious spirit by an appeal to fear and cupidity. Perhaps it would also cheer the Queen. 'Surely, my Lord,' he wrote, 'if you saw the wealth, the strength, the shipping and abundance of manners [manors] whereof these countries stand furnished, your heart would quake to think that so hateful an enemy as Spain should again be furnished with such instruments.'[10]

Enthusiasm was mutual. Leicester could hardly restrain his jubilation. 'There was such a noise, both in Delft, Rotterdam and Dort', he wrote, 'in crying "God save the Queen" as if one had been in Cheapside. . . . All sorts of people, from highest to lowest, assure themselves, now that they have Her Majesty's good countenance, to beat the Spaniards out of their country. Never were there people in such jollity as these be. I could be content to lose a limb could Her Majesty see these countries and towns as I have done.'[11]

Stupendous entertainment attended the new messiahs wherever they went. As they passed from Flushing to Middelburg, pigs were served on their feet, pheasants in their feathers, baked swans thrust their necks through enormous piecrusts, crystal castles of confectionery rose in sparkling magnificence, there was 'wine in abundance, variety of all sorts and wonderful welcomes'. Cannon roared, tar barrels blazed, bells pealed, dragons soared on fiery wings, wreaths of flowers descended and the visitors were deluged in cascades of endless Latin orations. At The Hague Peter, James and John met the Earl, and the Saviour walked upon the waves, ordering the disciples to cast their nets and present fish to His Excellency. Champions mounted upon whales tilted on the water, and the pageantry was interspersed with fireworks, charades and more orations. His Excellency was so far carried away as imprudently to declare, at Delft, that his family had been unjustly deprived of the crown of England. At Leyden 'a fair woman' representing the city 'fled the stage and leaping off hastily hid herself under the Earl's cloak'. Discreetly, His Excellency terminated the proceedings and 'led her to his lodging'.[12] Nothing like it had been seen since the days of Charles V. At Amsterdam Leicester figured as Joshua leading the Israelites into battle. But (not for the first time) the evening was marred by the prophet's attendants who, flown with wine, began tossing puddings out of the windows on to the heads of the assembled citizens below.

The wining and feasting postponed, but did not eliminate, the need for the major and ugly decision. Leicester's official title was that of the Queen's Lieutenant-General. Its meaning was obscure. What was his real function? If it was that of military commander, the appointment was plainly absurd. As the rhetorical but observant Wilford, one of the subordinate commanders, had declared of the Low Countries war: 'God hath stirred up this action to be a school to breed up soldiers to defend the freedom of England . . . a most fit school and nursery to nourish soldiers. . . .'[13] He was right. There were already a dozen seasoned veterans of high rank who had spent ten or more years learning their military trade in the Netherlands. Compared with them Leicester was an amateur. Was, then, his function political? In Leicester's mind the answer was unquestionably yes. Equally, the Netherlands envoys in England who had negotiated the Nonsuch Treaty and helped to arrange for its fulfilment were convinced that they were continuing the process of appointing a sovereign representative of the Queen, in spite of the disastrous experience with the Archduke Matthias and the Duke of Anjou. Their parting words to Leicester as he left England were to urge him 'to declare himself cheaf head and governor-general' of the Netherlands.[14]

But then there was the Queen, unpredictable, dictatorial and self-contradictory as ever. She had included in Leicester's instructions a series of peremptory orders. He was to reform the Netherlands constitution by increasing the powers of the States-General and diminishing the need for the deputies to refer back for orders to their provincial States. He was to reform their financial arrangements by enabling the States-General to levy taxes according to the 'advice of Her Majesty delivered to them by her lieutenant'. In short he was to create without delay the kind of unitary state that she – and Philip II – could understand. Yet at the same time she had specifically refused him permission to assume the sovereign authority necessary if he was to execute these orders – the authority which she herself had consistently refused to assume. In all the catastrophes that were to follow it is difficult to withhold some sympathy from a commander saddled with instructions so palpably contradictory, promised funds that never arrived, compelled to dig deep into his own pocket to supply his starving troops and furnished with only one experienced political adviser to steer him through a political jungle which was to bewilder far more experienced explorers. Basic to all calculations was the condition of his army – squalid, slovenly, untrained and virtually unclothed and unfed. Even in March 1586, three months after his arrival in Holland, Leicester could write to Burghley and Walsingham: 'there came no penny of treasure over since my coming hither . . . they perish for want of victuals and clothing in great numbers. The whole are ready to mutiny . . . I have let of my own more than I may spare.'[15]

Meanwhile Leicester had stepped into a perilous political quicksand. On New Year's Day 1586* a flourish of trumpets aroused him from his dressing-room. It heralded the arrival of deputies of all the States coming to offer him 'the name and place of Absolute Governor and General of all their forces and soldiers, with the disposition of their whole revenue and taxes'.[16] Then followed coy advances and retreats. But they were less the consequence of any fear of Leicester's that the offer might exceed his mistress's conception of his proper powers than that it would fall short of his own. 'Consider', he said to Davison, 'how advantageous to enemies

* By English or Old Style reckoning: 11 January, New Style.

that will seek holes in my coat, if I should take so great a name upon me and so little power.'[17] The crux of the matter was to decide who should elect the Council of State which was to advise him. By 24 January he had accepted an arrangement which gave him supreme command by land and sea and the power to nominate to all civil offices from lists of candidates submitted by the provincial States. Two weeks later, in the banqueting hall of the ancient palace of the Counts of Holland at The Hague, surrounded by William's heir, Maurice, and all the great officers of state, he was finally installed as Absolute Governor of the United States of the Netherlands.[18]

William Davison was dispatched to England to inform the Queen of the historic event. Unfortunately he was delayed by wind and weather until long after the news had reached the Queen by other channels. The result was an impressive explosion of royal fireworks which drove Burghley to his bed with a prudent attack of gout and prevented bolder spirits from obtaining any hearing of Leicester's case. A shower of advice descended upon the Absolute Governor from his friends at Court. Somehow the Queen's wrath had to be assuaged. 'Lay out two or three hundred crowns on some rare thing for a token to Her Majesty', urged Christopher Hatton, knowledgeable in such matters.[19]

Leicester's Netherlands crown proved to be a crown of thorns – 'as too manifest to us, in presenting to one of our subjects the same proposition which we had already declined . . .', as Elizabeth loftily observed to the States-General.[20] A rumour that Lady Leicester was joining her husband with a sumptuous train of retainers, ladies, coaches and side-saddles was the last straw. Cursing all who came near her, the Queen burst into a coloratura of 'extreme choler and dislike' at all Leicester's doings. Her dispatch to him was a set of variations on the theme of contempt for her royal person and her royal wisdom. Upon messengers like the faithful Davison, sent to present explanations, excuses and apologies, she merely heaped a shower of abuse. Her outbursts of rage had, for once, a kind of rationality. Before she had even begun to fulfil her promises to her new allies in hard cash, she was back on her former tack. It hardly needed Farnese's shrewd insight to see that the Nonsuch Treaty ran counter to all her traditional fear or reverence for Spain, to say nothing of an ingrained parsimony which turned the fearful costs of the war into a nightmare.

'Queen Elizabeth', Farnese wrote to Philip, 'is a woman: she is also by no means fond of expense. The Kingdom, accustomed to repose, is already weary of war: therefore they are all pacifically inclined.'[21] While Spain was well ahead with plans for the grand enterprise to invade England, Farnese was contriving his own scheme to 'chill the Queen in her plots, leagues and alliances and during the chill to carry forward their great design . . . to put the Queen to sleep'.[22]

It is far from clear what the true significance of these new negotiations with Spain – oblique, evasive and inconclusive – was. Certainly there was a strong element at Court, including Lord Cobham and Sir James Croft, the Comptroller, favourably disposed. Burghley, as usual, was sitting on the fence. Farnese himself believed that Burghley was a major obstruction to the flow of money and troops to Leicester, and certainly supplies were, for one reason or another, held back once more at this crucial moment. Champagny was likewise busily spreading rumours that the Queen was anxious for peace.

As spring passed into summer and the campaigning season reached its height, the affairs of both the opposing sides in the struggle turned to unutterable confusion. Outwardly, Leicester's position was less uncomfortable than it had been a few months earlier. The storm of royal wrath had at last blown itself out and supplies were beginning to come through. They were none too soon, for Farnese, already master of nearly the whole of Flanders and Brabant, launched an attack on the remaining strong points on the Maas which threatened his hold on Brabant. The first target was Grave, described by Lord North as 'the strongest town in all the Low Countries, though but a little one'.[23] But Farnese's attack was repelled and Leicester was thrown into ecstasies of elation. 'Oh that Her Majesty knew how easy a match she now hath with the King of Spain and what millions of afflicted people she had relieved in these countries.'[24] Amidst the feasting and banqueting the Governor was sending confident assurances to the Queen that he would quickly have Antwerp and Bruges back again.[25]

All these predictions miscarried sadly. Farnese, though pinched and pressed as hard as his English opponent, made an astonishing recovery. Grave was recaptured, and its fall was followed by the capture of all the other fortresses on the Maas. The governors of the cautionary towns, Flushing and The Brill, so vital to the north, bombarded Burghley with pleas for help. 'I can only cry for Flushing,' wrote Philip Sidney, 'but unless the moneys be sent over, there will be some terrible accident follow. . . .'[26] At The Brill, Thomas Cecil was disgusted with the quarrels and wranglings which now succeeded the premature enthusiasms in the Leicester camp. 'Our affairs here', he wrote to Burghley, his father, 'be such as that which we conclude overnight is broke in the morning; we agree not one with another but we are divided in many factions, so as if the enemy were as strong as we are factious and irresolute, we should make shipwreck of the cause this summer.'[27] It was lucky for Leicester that Farnese had his own troubles.

While Leicester was quarrelling with his commanders and the commanders were brawling amongst themselves, thousands of English troops still went unclothed and unfed.[28] Only the Irish auxiliaries suffered less than the rest. Clothes they scarcely missed, for they had never been accustomed to wear them. Clad only in a kilt, the Irish kern roamed the fens, living off the peasants, stealing and killing as he went. Sidney was outspoken in his condemnation of the waste of money and life involved in what masqueraded as economy and was in fact corruption. 'When soldiers grow to despair and give up towns, then it is too late to buy with hundred thousands what might have been saved with a trifle.'[29] Quartermaster Digges* amply confirmed Sidney's protest. 'I find the most part of the bands that came over in August and September more than half wasted, dead and gone, and many of the remainder sick, lame and shrewdly enfeebled . . . our soldiers . . . are so illcontented of their due for the time past, that, if pay come not speedily, before they be drawn to deal with the enemy, I doubt some worse adventure than I will divine beforehand.' Without training they would be more dangerous to their own leaders than to the enemy.[30]

But the Governor-General had other, more pressing things to attend to. He was steadily becoming submerged in a rising conflict that was to bedevil Netherlands politics for another century. As Lord North had remarked, the troubles with the Queen had

---

* Thomas Digges, an Oxford man, and a military engineer of great skill and energy. His father was Leonard Digges, the mathematician, who married Bridget, sister of Thomas Wilford (p. 90). The son of Thomas, Sir Dudley Digges (1589–1639), well known as a diplomat, lawyer and politician, inherited his father's energy and intelligence but not his honesty.

partially blown over, but amongst the Dutch they had left 'leaden heels and doubtful hearts'.[31] Without question, Leicester had also been the victim of the Queen's twisted diplomacy. His personal authority and the morale of his commanders and troops had been seriously undermined by the parsimony, the maladministration and the rumours of a deal with Spain for which, in the last analysis, she was responsible. Now in his weakness he allowed himself to be swept into a struggle between the two parties which had emerged from the Netherlands rebellion.

Everywhere, but especially in Holland, there was a continuity of persons and even of ethos between the urban oligarchy and the old ruling class. The men who had assumed control of the town governments were the 'libertinists'. They were in no sense enthusiasts for Calvinism. At the most they had adapted themselves to the Reformation; they were anti-confessional, in the Erasmian tradition. The founding of the University at Leyden in thanksgiving for the ending of the siege in 1574 made the city a strong centre of libertinist humanism. It was to be found in other cities like Haarlem and Delft, but the mingled humanism and anti-theocratic temper of Leyden was unique. It was characteristic of the prevailing spirit of toleration that Pieter Adriaan van der Werff, an elder of the Reformed Church and one of the burgomasters who had led the resistance during the siege, insisted on his right to send his son to a school kept by a Roman Catholic schoolmaster, rejecting the clamour raised by the rigid Calvinists. His colleague and town secretary, Jan van Hout, tried unsuccessfully to transfer responsibility for the care of the town poor entirely into secular hands. (Normally this powerful means of proselytising among the masses was jointly administered by church and secular authorites.) Tension between Calvinists and anti-Calvinists was acute. 'Rather the Spanish Inquisition', declared one anti-Calvinist at Leyden, 'than the Genevan discipline, that poxy old whore.'[32]

As one or two of the more perceptive English visitors to the Low Countries noted, the libertinists were chiefly concerned to preserve their freedom from a threat of Calvinist theocracy. In this respect they were following in the footsteps of Orange. Yet whereas he had succeeded in retaining a large measure of support from the common people (including those of the south) the gap between latitudinarian oligarchy and Calvinist democracy now

began to widen. In the larger towns the struggle for power swayed
backwards and forwards between the parties. The popular leaders
of the Calvinist democratic theocracy were often drawn from refugees from the south. In the city of Utrecht, which increasingly
became Leicester's centre of action, affairs fell into the hands of
three immigrants: Daniel de Borchgrave, a Fleming who became
his private secretary and interpreter; Gerard Proninck (known as
Deventer), a Brabanter, whose political ambitions had brought
him the burgomastership of Utrecht; last, and most dubious
member of the triumvirate, Jan Reingout, also a Brabanter and a
former servant of Granvelle, Alba and Requesens. Their influence
over the stream of refugees coming from Flanders, Brabant and
the Walloon provinces into the north was powerful. Utrecht in
particular was being strongly Calvinised even before Leicester's
arrival. Swiftly the Queen's governor found himself the leader (or
instrument) of the extreme Calvinist faction in the Netherlands.
In one city after another – Utrecht, Leyden, Amsterdam, Medem-
blik, Enkhuizen – Leicester was believed to be implicated in plots
by the extreme Calvinist faction to seize control of the government.
Once again, as with John Casimir at Ghent a few years earlier, the
Queen's name and patronage were linked with the activities of a
party of fanatics whose fellows in England were an object of utmost
detestation to her.

There was a powerful economic undertow to all this. The
Utrecht democrats particularly resented the wealth which came
Holland's way through her trade with the enemy. The year 1586
was one of famine food prices following a bad harvest. The
southern provinces were especially badly affected. The southerners
round Leicester were probably sincere in their conviction that if
Holland would cut off food supplies, Farnese's position would
become untenable and surrender would inevitably follow. The
Hollanders maintained with equal conviction that if they stopped
victualling the south, it would be fed from other sources. Holland
would merely lose the revenues which enabled her to finance the
major share of the war costs.[33] Thus religion, economics and
politics combined to breed a sharp antagonism between the oligarchs and democrats, with Leicester playing the part of the
Protestant demagogue. The first victim was one of the firmest
Dutch Anglophiles, the man whose friendship Leicester had
persistently sought and whom he had earlier pronounced to be 'in

ability above all men' – Paul Buys, former Advocate of Holland. Now, overnight, Buys became (in Leicester's words) 'a very dangerous man . . . a lewd sinner . . . very knave, a traitor, . . . a hater of the Queen and of all the English . . . a bolsterer of all papists and ill men, a dissembler, a devil, an atheist . . . a most naughty man and a most notorious drunkard in the worst degree'. His Netherlands allies as a whole were dismissed with a lordly flourish as 'churls and tinkers', at best 'bakers and brewers'. In August Buys was thrown into prison, and though Leicester denied responsibility for having ordered the arrest, he refused to release him.

At the end of September came the attack on Zutfen, a rash and pointless failure in which Leicester's nephew Sidney received the wounds from which he died soon after. Since July the general confusion had grown worse. Bartholomew Clerk, one of the Governor's two English counsellors, a caricature of an academic in miniature, could stand it no longer. 'I beseech your good Lordship', he wrote to Burghley, 'to consider what a hard case it is for a man . . . who was a public Reader in the University [of Oxford] (and therefore cannot be young) to come now among the guns and drums, tumbling up and down, day and night, over waters and banks, dykes and ditches . . . hearing many insolences with silence . . . a course most different from my nature and most unmeet for him that hath ever profound learning.'[34] The plaintive Clerk was allowed to go home. Thomas Wilkes, who replaced him, was of altogether tougher fibre. But by this time the incessant quarrels of Dutch and English, Dutch and Dutch, and above all English and English had worn out even Leicester. In May he had written to Walsingham in a mood of gloomy exhaustion from his encampment at Arnhem: 'I am weary, indeed I am weary, Mr Secretary.'[35] As the campaigning season ended in November he took his farewell of the States, bearing with him from Flushing their parting gift of thankfulness (or relief) for his exit, a silver-gilt case 'as tall as a man'.

No sooner was he out of the way than there occurred another disastrous proof of Leicester's total lack of judgement. Immediately after the skirmish at Zutfen Sir William Pelham had captured Deventer, a flourishing centre of trade, and a known supply depot for the Spaniards at Zutfen, for it contained a predominantly Catholic population. With maladroit genius, Leicester had in-

stalled as its protector Sir William Stanley, a Catholic soldier of
fortune who had fought as a mercenary for Alba. Stanley commanded a garrison of twelve hundred Irish Catholic kerns of
terrifying aspect and habits. 'It seemed', said an observer, 'that
they belonged not to Christendom but to Brazil.'[36] Simultaneously
the command of the fort overlooking Zutfen was given to Rowland
Yorke, a mercenary desperado who had fought on both sides and
was always ready to desert any employer for higher pay. In
Leicester's eyes he possessed one sovereign merit: he was the
sworn enemy of John Norris, for whom Leicester cherished a
cordial hatred.

Norris, Wilkes and the States-General made immediate protest:
all to no purpose. At Deventer a reign of terror ensued. It was
ended only in January 1587 by the treason of Stanley and Yorke
who surrendered Deventer and Zutfen fort to the enemy. Perfect
Walrus and Carpenter, the erring captains 'wept with the burghers
for company'. They had acted (they said) not with 'covetous mind
for profit' but only for the discharge of conscience and the love
of God. 'It is now said', wrote Sir John Conway to Walsingham,
'he [Stanley] hath and shall have £30,000.'[37]

The effect of the treason was to destroy any remaining confidence between the Dutch and their English allies and transmute
the faltering morale of Farnese and his forces into high jubilation.
For the first time Oldenbarneveldt, Advocate of Holland, emerges
as the authoritative political leader of the Dutch nation, brush-
ing aside the authority of the absent Absolute Governor and
entrusting special military powers to Prince Maurice, now
Stadholder of Holland. A barrage of abuse and recrimination
was exchanged between The Hague and Greenwich, where the
Queen was now at odds with all her Council, including even
Burghley. Only Leicester was back in favour, beating his
breast, echoing the Queen's resolve that he should never return
to the Low Countries, and finally departing to Bath to drink the
waters.[38]

In his stead, on what was called a mission of expostulation, went
Lord Buckhurst. After a frightening crossing, three days and
nights at sea 'miserably sick and in great danger of drowning',
he arrived at Flushing at the end of March. But making an
instantaneous recovery, he made haste to send home demands for
immediate relief for the Queen's starving soldiers 'for Jesus' sake'.

Buckhurst, sincere, sympathetic but firm, managed to spread confidence and calm as surely as Leicester had spread mischief and hysteria.

His assessment of the political situation was shrewd and remarkably accurate. The Protestants and Puritans in the rebellious provinces (he calculated) did not exceed one in five.[39] The rebellion was only possible because it comprehended Catholics and Protestants and the uncommitted; it was for 'their country and liberty only' and directed against Spanish tyranny. Hence the need for England to act, in her own defence as well as in that of the Dutch. How often had Elizabeth heard the same truth from Orange?[40] While Wilkes continued loyally to defend the absent Leicester's conception of his office and his responsibility to the 'commonalty', Buckhurst patiently worked out the terms of a new agreement with the Dutch. Holland and Zeeland voted an extra £100,000 for the war. Would the Queen contribute £50,000? The war, Buckhurst pleaded eloquently, passionately, was for the defence of England. It was no use. 'No reason that breedeth charges', Walsingham wrote to him laconically, 'can in any sort be digested.'[41] Buckhurst was ordered, on the contrary, to urge upon the Dutch once more the merits of making peace with Spain. Faithfully he did his duty. The only effect was – as he had predicted – to make Anglo-Dutch relations even worse. It was plain by June that his mission, like many earlier ones, had been turned into a farce by the Queen's tortuous diplomacy. Furthermore Leicester, disastrously rested and restored in health and spirits, had decided to return to his post. It was time for his critics to go. Norris and Wilkes, fearing the worst, did not wait for Leicester to return but made their getaway. 'I shall stay to be dandled with no love-days nor leave-takings,' as the departing Wilkes remarked to Walsingham.[42] More manfully, Buckhurst waited for Leicester's return in July and stood his ground against the stream of vituperation that was poured out on him by the Absolute Governor. Then he returned home to receive his reward: imprisonment in his country house on the Queen's orders. He was luckier than the unfortunate Wilkes, now, after much faithful service to Leicester, described by his master as 'a villain, a devil without faith or religion' and immediately thrown into the Fleet prison on the Queen's orders. Norris got off lightly: to be forbidden the Queen's presence cannot at this stage have been an

unmixed punishment.* Leicester's second mission proved, if anything, more catastrophic than the first. Intrigues with the Calvinist,
anti-States party continued at Utrecht, Leyden and elsewhere,
but too clumsily to avoid discovery and defeat. The crowning
failure was the loss of Sluys to Farnese in August. The blame could
be fairly divided between the States and the English, but if 'The
inaction of the States was one of the causes of its loss . . . distrust
of Leicester was the cause of the inaction'.[43] It seems fair comment.
By another unlikely victory, Farnese had acquired a valuable base
for the invasion of England, the plans for which were slowly
maturing in Spain. At the year's end the Absolute Governor took
his final departure. It was none too soon. He left the territories
which had been entrusted to his care in a state of civil war. For
this he was entirely responsible and entirely, eloquently, even
piously, unrepentant. 'God send me a wind to blow me from them
all. These legs of mine shall never go again to Holland. Let the
States get others to serve their mercenary turn, for me they shall
not have.'[44] He arranged for a medal to be struck in his own
honour. The device was a flock of sheep guarded by an English
mastiff; the motto, *Non gregem sed ingratos*. The Dutch riposted
promptly and with relish. They produced a coin showing an ape
smothering her young; on the reverse a man 'falling into the fire'
in his efforts to avoid the smoke: *Fugiens fumum, incidit in ignem*.

The military, political and financial disasters of the Leicester
period need not be laboured again. They have been set out in
detail many times.[45] At a cost of something between £125,000 and
£150,000 a year, or roughly a half of her ordinary income, Elizabeth had been drawn into an apparently endless conflict. The
corruption and confusion was bottomless: the visible product a
half-naked, underfed, mutinous mob of Pistols and Bardolphs,
wasting away at a rate that put the Queen into a perpetual state
of alarm over an enterprise into which she had been drawn un-
willingly and without conviction.

The immediate cause of the disasters was the Earl of Leicester
himself. He has been trounced, roundly and rightly, by Sir John
Neale.[46] A dutiful contemporary anticipated his judgement. 'He
is not so facile to forget as ready to revenge,' wrote Thomas

---

* It was not Wilkes's first taste of royal gratitude. In 1574 he had been left
to face the wrath of Catherine de Medici in Paris when Elizabeth's plan to
support Alençon was uncovered.

Wilkes. 'My very heavy and mighty adversary will disgrace and undo me.'[47] Leicester represented all that was worst in the politics and culture of the English Renaissance. But, like Duke Casimir, he returned to England to receive immediate reward for his political ineptitude and military incompetence. In his charge the Queen placed the land defence against the Armada. Never had he been so cock-a-hoop, so full of pious clichés, so high in the royal favour. It was fortunate for England that his military skill was not to be tested a second time.

On the other hand, the Queen has never lacked defenders. Her financial anxieties have been stressed. The budgetary surplus achieved between 1572 and 1585 thereafter disappeared, to be replaced by the virtual bankruptcy of her last years. Hence the involuted intrigues for peace with Farnese, the diplomatic quadrilles that puzzled and dismayed her most loyal servants as much as they did her expectant allies. Time and again her servants and advisers of all complexions had warned her against the false economies by which her financial surplus of the seventies and eighties had been harvested. Walsingham, Sidney, Thomas Cecil, Wilford, Norris and a dozen others had warned her of the consequences of cheeseparing when vital military decisions were at stake. All in vain: as Professor Wernham has said, she was not a military leader. She failed totally to understand the process by which victories are achieved. Having finally taken the plunge in 1585, she had appointed Leicester as Lieutenant-General. (The appointment was her responsibility and no one else's.) Why? Because he was the right man for the post? Or because he was the object of a long, passionate private relationship? There can be no quibble over this. At the crucial moment Elizabeth was guilty of a disastrous compromise between her private passions and public needs; worse still, between the demands of her natural parsimony and those of the public weal. Ironically, the truth comes out of the mouth of Walsingham in an apologetic dispatch to Leicester himself in April. He was sorry, he confessed, that the Privy Council wrote to the Queen's Governor of the Low Countries so infrequently, but there was a simple cause – 'Her Majesty, *retaining the whole direction of the causes of that country to herself and such advice as she receiveth underhand*, they know not what to write or advise.' He continued: 'If to offend all the world be a good cause of government then can we do not amiss. . . . I never found her less disposed to take a course of prevention of the approaching mischiefs towards this realm than at this present. And, to be plain with you, *there is none here that hath either credit or courage to deal effectually with her in any of her great causes.*' (My italics.)[48]

Leicester had one recommendation for the post of Governor of the Netherlands, and only one. Conceited, quarrelsome, ungrateful, disloyal, jealous, stupid and corrupt he might be; but he was very rich, and in the cause of his ambition he was prepared to pour out generous libations from his private fortune. That was enough for the Queen. Let Buckhurst have the last word when he wrote of the Governorship: 'It had been better bestowed upon a meaner man of more skill.'[49] I have shown earlier that such men existed. It was the Queen's own candidate who had (as Geyl wrote) compromised every cause which he had sponsored.[50] This was the reality of the Tudor despotism in foreign affairs.

Inadvertently, but only so, the future constitution of the Dutch Republic emerged from the follies and failures of English policy in the seventies and eighties. The lingering obsession for a foreign sovereign which had characterised Netherlands politics and diplomacy for twenty years was at last dispelled. Under Oldenbarneveldt and Maurice of Nassau the States could set their feet on a path towards genuine independence. The most that could be said for the English intervention before the Armada was that, in spite of the betrayals and failures, it had probably helped to slow down Farnese's advance northwards. More important, the lessons learnt at terrible cost by the English commanders were to be increasingly valuable during the next twenty years.

The events of 1587 – the loss of Deventer, Zutfen fort and Sluys – once again showed how fluid the military situation was, how small was the gap separating victory from defeat, how closely the contingencies of war were related to human capacity and human failings. The opposing armies were both the victims of maladministration and the inevitable mutinies that followed in its wake.[51] But now the military scene was to change. From the middle of August 1587 the decisive action was to be not on land but on the sea.

The story of the Armada has been told many times.[52] In our context it is necessary only to refer to a few salient features that have sometimes been unwittingly or wittingly obscured in patriotic writings. The design of the grand enterprise was to gather an invasion force on the Flemish coast under Parma, who would be strongly reinforced from Italy. Santa Cruz, the veteran of Lepanto, with the Armada, was to make rendezvous with Parma and act as convoy to his invasion force. Historians' opinions on the merits of the plan have varied widely. 'In some ways,' Mattingley wrote, 'it was a good plan.'[53] 'A mad enterprise' was Geyl's comment.[54] Before choosing between these two alternatives, let us note that the plan was very different in execution from conception. By the time the Armada sailed, Santa Cruz was dead. He was replaced by Medina Sidonia, whose experience of naval affairs was nil. Second, the fleet that sailed comprised only half Santa Cruz's original demands in terms of naval strength and less than a third in terms of fighting men.[55] Third, and most important, the strategy was fundamentally different from that originally devised by Santa Cruz. That was a plan for the direct invasion of England from Spain. Later a new, most hazardous and crucial phase was introduced into the operation – the attempted junction of the Spanish fleet with Parma's invasion force in the Netherlands. Yet the details of the rendezvous were left unbelievably vague. One of Parma's emissaries sent to Madrid on the eve of the expedition pointed out a fatal flaw. Parma had no deep-water port in Flanders. Spanish galleons drawing twenty-five to thirty feet could not approach anywhere near Dunkirk, which with Nieupoort sheltered the invasion force and Parma's fleet of flat-bottomed canal barges. Why not give up the project now and save time and money? Parma and his emissary were ignored. 'Four ships of war could sink every one of my boats,' Parma warned Philip.[56] The grand plan took no account of the sandbanks and shallows that lined the entire coast where the rendezvous was to take place. It ignored the perils from the prevailing westerly winds which blew on to a lee shore, making disembarkation difficult enough in normal conditions and suicidal in battle. Finally, it disregarded completely the large fleet of nimble men-of-war based on Flushing which patrolled the entire Flemish coast and Scheldt estuary under Justin of Nassau, the illegitimate son of William the Silent. In one dispatch after another, Parma tried to explain to Philip the impossible hazards of the revised operation. His representations were totally ignored.

Leicester, now commander of the anti-invasion strategy in

England, was without even the framework of a supply organisation. He was desperately short of officers, weapons and trained troops. 'I am sorry,' wrote Walsingham, 'so great a danger hanging over this realm so slightly regarded and so carelessly provided for. . . .'[57] So the insouciance of Philip was matched only by that of England. When the tortuous English peace negotiations with Spain were finally broken off in mid-July, the Spanish Armada was at the mouth of the English Channel. By the end of July, when the Spaniards were at Calais roads, not one Spanish ship had been sunk by gunfire. The Dutch fleet under Justin of Nassau and part of the English fleet under Lord Henry Seymour were patrolling the Flanders and Zeeland coast quite independently, without liaison, indeed without the faintest knowledge of each other's strength or function. If at this stage the Armada could have made its way into Flushing or Antwerp the threat might have been fatal.

It was fortunate for Medina Sidonia that Anglo-Dutch operations were as uncoordinated as those between his Armada and Parma. Only a brilliant last-moment improvisation of Drake's fireships saved a situation in which the allied fleet ran out of ammunition. The eleventh-hour rescue was due to the resource and inspiration of individual English commanders, combined with Anglo-Dutch control of the Continental seaboard from Flanders to Zeeland. A favourable wind allowed the Armada to avoid complete disaster on the Flanders sands, and two-thirds escaped northwards. But at no time did the professionals regard it as a great English victory. They knew only too well how vulnerable they were. So did Walsingham: 'So our half-doing doth breed dishonour and leave the disease uncured!'[58]

As early as 5 August Leicester was ordered to discharge a third of his infantry from Tilbury – three days before the Queen made her triumphal visit. On the ninth Burghley was satisfied that the Armada had been blown north and would not return. He was evidently itching to make a start on naval demobilisation too. The following day Walsingham had remarked Elizabeth's 'conceit' that she ought to stay at Tilbury in case the enemy should attempt something. But then he added, no doubt still smarting from the Queen's displeasure: 'But presently she changed her mind. Thus your Lordship [Burghley] seeth that this place breedeth courage. I fear now more the hand of God in respect of unseasonableness of the weather than the enemy.' He need not have worried. By the time Elizabeth, at Tilbury, delivered her most famous speech of all, the danger was past. Roger Williams, that indefatigable Welsh soldier of fortune, was probably right when he declared that 'miracles alone had saved England from perdition'.[59] They had also snatched away from Parma and his decimated, emaciated troops rotting in Dunkirk and Nieupoort their best, and as events were to prove, their last, remaining chance of subjugating either England or the new Republic.

6 Relations Transformed

IT is a commonplace irony of history that a political alliance can often withstand any strain except the victory it is designed to achieve. If the truth of this was not immediately verified by the Anglo-Dutch defeat of the Armada it was partly because few contemporaries saw it as in any sense the final or decisive triumph over Spain which it seemed to some later chroniclers. There was certainly an unprecedented itch, on the English side anyway, to be rid of Nonsuch and its costly alliance, which seemed to point straight to bankruptcy. For once the Queen was united with her Council, including even Walsingham, in wishing the Treaty at the bottom of the sea. But it was not so easily done. 'I wish our fortune and theirs were not so straitly tied as it is,' observed Walsingham regretfully, 'so that we cannot well untie without great hazard.'[1]

In the Netherlands the interlude of cordiality that celebrated the Protestant triumph was shortlived. Leicester's successor, the brave Lord Willoughby, was a better soldier and a better man than his predecessor. But the legacy of confusion and mistrust which Leicester had left behind him was too much for his impetuous nature. It was not long before he too was at loggerheads with both Oldenbarneveldt and Maurice. Without reluctance he made way for Sir Francis Vere, a commander of exceptional ability whose cousin he had married.[2]

In the wake of the brief glory of 1588 injury piled upon injury, failure upon failure. A freebooting expedition to Spain and Portugal in April 1589, thinly disguised as a project to restore to his rights Don Antonio, pretender to the Portuguese crown,* was an expensive failure. It lost six or seven thousand Dutch and English troops and won nothing.

In the same month – as if Deventer, the English betrayal and Zutfen were not enough – the important city of Geertruidenberg, north of Breda, was surrendered to the Spaniards by its mutinous

---

* Don Antonio, prior of Crato, had first made his appearance, in a condition of starvation, in Paris immediately after the assassination of William the Silent. Leicester had suggested him as a promising successor to Anjou and William as Governor of the Netherlands.

English garrison. Its commander, Sir John Wingfield, was Willoughby's brother-in-law. Bitterly indignant, Oldenbarneveldt and the States issued a list of names of those responsible for the treason, putting a price on every head and ordaining that when captured they should be hanged without trial. The list was headed by the name of Wingfield. Thus animosities multiplied. There was bitter resentment at the English Court at what was regarded as a monstrous injustice to Wingfield; at the continued Dutch trading with the enemy; at the contemptuous treatment by Olden-barneveldt of the English members of the Council of State. The States, in their turn, kept green the memory of the insults suffered at the hands of the Leicester régime and the near civil war in which it had ended, the betrayals, the Queen's broken promises, the high-handed behaviour of the English diplomats and the un-biddable arrogance of the English commanders. Disenchantment seemed complete.

Yet behind the clamour of accusation and counter-accusation, a subtle but profound change in the relationship between the two states was taking place. The Queen knew that in her own best interest she could not desert her ally, who in the spring of 1589 was still facing a threat from Parma which seemed on the face of it to be more serious than any so far. With three or four soldiers to every one of his opponents, Parma seemed poised to break through the entire Maas-Waal river line placed in his hands by the betrayal of Deventer, Zutfen and Geertruidenberg. The risk of a break-through to Amsterdam and the Zuyder Zee from the east seemed acute. The English civilians on the Dutch Council were cast into deepest apprehensions. 'The state of these Provinces', wrote Thomas Bodley,* one of the English delegates to the Dutch Council of State, 'is weaker than it hath been these many years, and unless by Her Majestie's extraordinary assistance and counsel it be presently holpen, there is little appearance that they can hold it out long.'[3] George Gilpin was equally gloomy. 'These afflicted countries,' he wrote to Willoughby from The Hague, 'never stood in more fickle and dangerous terms, the enemy being ready with great force . . . and themselves never more unready to withstand them.'[4]

---

* Bodley came from a Protestant Devon family who had fled to Geneva in Mary's reign. He became a Fellow of Merton College, Oxford. Posterity has rightly assessed his contribution to learning – the Bodleian Library – as of greater consequence than the diplomatic services for which he was honoured by the Queen.

But for once Providence was kind. The attack was postponed by Parma's illness. Until July he was on leave with the dropsy. No sooner had he recovered than there was another disruptive mutiny of his troops in August. By the time order was restored Henry III had been assassinated in France, and Henry of Navarre was rapidly establishing his authority. The situation in France now became a matter of acute anxiety to Spain. The hard winter of 1589-90 that froze all the canals and rivers facing Parma was no help. The Spanish war effort was even more solidly congealed – by mutiny, by shortage of pay, food, weapons and ammunition.[5]

Reproaching Philip bitterly, Parma finally accepted his orders to divert his energies to France. With 12,000 foot and 3,000 horse he left for the relief of Paris, accompanied by a number of his former opponents from the ranks of the Walloon nobility – Aerschot, Aremberg, Chimay, Berlaymont and others. Sick to death though he was, he scored an immediate success, but no sooner did he turn back to Brussels than Henry IV renewed his assault. Thereafter Parma was preoccupied with the Franco-Spanish struggle in Normandy and Brittany. Just as in 1572, the Netherlands had once again been saved by events in France. In July 1592, unaware of the fate Philip was preparing for him, surrounded by his Walloon commanders, noisy, quarrelsome and selfish as ever, he was dispatching pious relics to enrich his master's collection in the Escorial – the left leg of the glorious St Philip, the shrunken head of the glorious martyr St Lawrence. But by December he was dead, destroyed by Philip as surely as Rommel was to be destroyed by Hitler.

Brilliant, audacious to the end, he had never recaptured the momentum of his thrust in the eighties northwards and westwards. He had shown what was in Philip's eyes a culpable lack of enthusiasm for the enterprise against England. His successes had been scintillating but shockingly expensive in troops and bribes. In the Netherlands and Spain his enemies poisoned the minds of Philip and his officials against him. Champagny, now crippled with gout but as mischievous as ever, hated Parma as much as Parma detested Champagny. He was, Parma had said, 'un instrument diabolique, mal intentionné et perfide'.[6] Champagny alleged that only one-tenth of the funds provided from Spain were spent on their proper purposes. The rest (he asserted) were adroitly

E

disbursed by Parma's servants and dependants to other servants, dependants, relatives and mistresses.[7]

Now the military and political initiative moved from Spain to the Dutch Republic, where a powerful partnership had been forged between Oldenbarneveldt, Advocate of the States of Holland, and Maurice of Nassau. Through a skilful move by Oldenbarneveldt, Maurice now became Stadholder in five of the seven provinces. He also had the loyal support of his cousin, William Louis, Stadholder of Friesland and later of the remaining northerly provinces. The last decade of the century was an astonishing period in which rapid economic growth, political consolidation and a series of skilful, if hard-won, military victories were all combined under the leadership of the Advocate and the two Princes, at this stage all still united in understanding.

In the year of the Armada Maurice had just attained his majority. His cousin, William Louis, son of old John Nassau of Gelderland, was seven years older. Oldenbarneveldt, nearly twice Maurice's age, was the senior partner. Born in the province of Utrecht, Oldenbarneveldt had been largely educated overseas. He came as a stranger to Holland, but he dedicated to its struggle for independence all that tenacious political genius which made him one of the great figures of the age. He shared all Leicester's belief in autocratic method, and his optimism, but combined them with an inexhaustible capacity for work and a subtle intelligence. While Oldenbarneveldt managed financial and diplomatic affairs virtually single-handed, military operations were left largely to Maurice. The Advocate's method was to exploit to the utmost his position as the political chief of the province of Holland, providing as it did something between a half and two-thirds of the war budget of the loosely federal Republic. The fact that each deputy was limited by the brief he received from his provincial States left comfortable room for the Advocate's manœuvres. In this way the States-General became again the centre of the constitution, symbolised in the person of the Advocate. By an acute irony, the unitary State which Elizabeth had demanded, and which her Governor, Leicester, had sought through a Calvinist Caesarism, was now achieved by the leader of the States party who had been one of its principal opponents. The Council of State, in which the Queen's representatives had so far played an important role, declined proportionately in status. As early as 1589 the Queen had to resign herself to its serving as a merely advisory body, and recognising the authority of the States-General and provincial States as the 'absolute governors'. In the obstinacy of Oldenbarneveldt the Queen at last met her match.[8]

The object of these new political arrangements was plain: to secure the absolute independence of the northern provinces from Spain, France or England. To this end, Oldenbarneveldt manipulated relations between the States-General and the other organs of government so as to maintain something verging on dictatorial powers, and harness the rapidly growing economic wealth of the north to the needs of the war. It does not follow, however, that he had yet abandoned more ambitious schemes of recovering the south, as the events of 1600 were to show.[9] In many respects, but especially economic, Oldenbarneveldt was in a much more fortunate position than William the Silent had ever been. William had been compelled to seek and accept any crumbs of external help he could get. Externally and internally, the situation gave Oldenbarneveldt the chance of far greater freedom of manœuvre as regards England and France than William could ever have hoped for.

As the military instrument of Oldenbarneveldt's plans, Maurice of Nassau was the antithesis of Parma. Still barely out of his teens, he deserved the title of 'silent' more than his father – an odd, withdrawn, cryptic youth, who had studied mathematics, and especially the mathematics of war, at Leyden. His master was the great Simon Stevin, another of the many refugees from the south who helped to lay the foundations of the culture of the north. After the disaster of Geertruidenberg, Maurice was already prepared with detailed plans for a general counter-attack based on a series of military reforms which were to revolutionise European techniques of warfare. His basic principle was to increase the firepower of infantry and cavalry alike: fewer pikes, more harquebuses and muskets. But his greatest concentration of effort was still on the technique of siege. Not only his sappers but his infantry were now armed with spades. It has been said, with some justice, that the spade was Maurice's prime weapon. With Oldenbarneveldt's help the whole organisation of the army, especially its pay and discipline, was reformed. For Maurice had seen that the failures of Alba, Parma and Leicester alike derived from the failure of morale: no pay, no fight. The yield of the convoy and licence duties had already begun the increase which was to double this source of war revenue in the decade after the Armada. This was the economic base on which Maurice and William Louis were able to build their strategy for an offensive war. It centred on the use of towns as fortified supply depots. From these, over-whelming force could quickly be deployed at the point of attack where it was most needed.[10] Thus in one way or another the Dutch genius for minute, accurate scientific observation, already brilliantly applied to zoology, microscopy, astronomy, anatomy, architecture and painting, was now applied with equal success to the arts of war. Maurice's military genius was (in Motley's phrase) 'passionless as algebra'; in politics he has been called 'the perfect chessmaster'.*

Far from reducing the importance of the Anglo-Dutch alliance, the rise of the new diarchy effectively increased it. William Louis's estimate of the size of army needed for victory under the reformed concepts of war was 8500 infantry and 1500 cavalry. But the greater part of this field army until 1589 was to be English. So were some of the best of the officers. As Thomas Wilford had predicted,† the Netherlands wars had proved a splendid school for English officers. Behind Maurice stood a closely related group of commanders – Sir Francis and Horace Vere, Roger Williams, Thomas Morgan, John and Edward Norris and many others. The Veres were Essex gentry, descended from the Earls of Oxford, who had long owned a string of villages and manors along the Colne and Stour.[11]

Francis was the George Patton-crossed-with-Montgomery of Maurice's campaigns: fiery, arrogant, but clear-headed; a great commander. His *Commentaries* are a supremely self-confident, not to say self-congratulatory, account of some of his great actions. As his editor wrote:

> And what his Sword indited, that his Pen
> With like success doth here fight o're agen:
> What Mars performed Mercurie doth tell;
> None e're but Cesar fought and wrote so well.
> Why may not then his Book this title carry
> The second part of *Cesar's Commentary*?[12]

His autobiography at any rate ensured that his merits have not been undervalued by historians.[13] He was not loved by Maurice but his leadership was indispensable: he fought and commanded

* But on Maurice's neglect of field intelligence, see p. 119.
† See Ch. 5, p. 91.

in all the great actions from Leicester's fiascos down to the Truce of 1609. More than any other English commanders, 'the fighting Veres' symbolised the steady professionalisation of the English command in the Low Countries.[14]

John Norris was of an earlier vintage and one of the numerous victims of Leicester's mingled spite and incompetence. If his valour had been tinctured with any diplomatic or political capacity he might well have been Elizabeth's choice as commander-in-chief; but of any such diplomatic sophistication Norris was totally innocent. He remained a fighting soldier, one of that brave, high-handed, quarrelsome band of brothers whom Fuller called the *pulli martis* – 'so great their states and stomachs that they often jostled with others'.[15]

His second-in-command, Roger Williams, was in many respects very like his chief but, as befitted his race, a great deal more articulate. There are few more lively reports on the Netherlands wars than his dispatches. Like Norris, he quarrelled with Leicester and later attached himself to Essex. He ended his days in the French wars, still talking bawdy with the Queen. Thomas Morgan, a fellow Welshman, had been in the wars since the first capture of The Brill in 1572. After that he was in action at Haarlem, Antwerp, Flushing, Rheinberg and Bergen-op-Zoom. 'A very sufficient, gallant gentleman', wrote Lord Willoughby, who had no particular liking for him, adding – strange epitaph for a Welshman – 'but unfurnished of language'. Like a number of English, Welsh and Scottish officers, Morgan married a Dutch wife, the daughter of Baron van Merode, who after his death married the illegitimate sailor son of William the Silent, Justin of Nassau.[16]

With all these subordinate but indispensable English commanders Maurice and Oldenbarneveldt managed to maintain businesslike if not always cordial relations. They were vital to the counter-actions of the 1590s. In England, all but a handful of disgruntled and disappointed seekers after military preferment agreed that the Netherlands of Prince Maurice and the Veres was a prime nursery of good soldiers.[17]

The civil counterpart of these military changes in civil affairs was an alteration in the English representation on the Dutch Council of State. Thomas Bodley, the sitting member, was high-handed and overbearing, though to do him justice, he seems to have been unaware of it, preening himself on his skill in redeeming Leicester's 'insolent demeanour' towards the Dutch. Unfortunately the Dutch disliked him; the Queen hardly less so. She wished, she declared 'for his comfort he were hanged'. But he survived till 1596, when he retired, finding the work of the Council – now virtually an advisory body without executive power – unrewarding and frustrating. The new member, Gilpin, was equable and amiable, a competent company secretary, but if his talents were unimpressive, he had the (by now) almost unique merit amongst the Queen's agents of being liked by the Dutch. For one thing he spoke their language, an accomplishment almost as rare then as it is now. He was therefore able to take his turn as chairman of the Council of State.

These changes, taking place in the wake of the defeat of the Armada and the withdrawal of Parma to France, signified more than merely an alteration in personal and constitutional relations. They spelt the end of the ideas of Dutch dependency, of the Netherlands as a protectorate, which had hag-ridden Anglo-Dutch relations for nearly twenty years.

By October 1589 the Privy Council, vaguely conscious of the new relationship, reconciled themselves to the fact that there was no English soldier of adequate rank capable of fulfilling the politico-military task which had defeated Leicester and Willoughby. In the spring of 1590 discussion still turned on the possibility of Buckhurst going as a purely political agent to the Netherlands – 'a person of quality, wise and temperate and grateful to the States'. Willoughby himself esteemed Buckhurst highly: 'To win and retain the States wholly to be ours, no so fit a person as my Lord Buckhurst most agreeable to them.'[18] All of which was very true; but as the sceptical Walsingham pointed out to Bodley, Buckhurst 'might have done much had he come upon the Queen's first resolution'. Now, as usual, the time had slipped by and it was too late. Bodley agreed.[19] In the end, for reasons that are obscure, it was Thomas Wilkes, not Buckhurst, who went. Francis Vere became, in effect, commander-in-chief of the English forces, subject only to Prince Maurice. Willoughby, still bitter over what he thought was the Dutch slander of his brother-in-law, Wingfield, was glad to leave.[20]

Elizabeth had already sampled Oldenbarneveldt's quality. In 1589 he led a delegation to England. His situation was delicate.

The Queen was more sensitive than ever to the Dutch policy of trading with the enemy. Their argument – if we don't supply the Spaniards somebody else will – was totally unacceptable to an England threatened not merely by one Armada but by several, all fitted out with naval stores supplied by her Dutch ally. Oldenbarneveldt riposted with protests at the piratical raids by their English ally on Dutch shipping. Yet somehow the storm blew over. One reason was that a revived threat to England could again be conjured up in France. The growing strength of Henry of Navarre was all very well, but might it not portend French sovereignty stretching all round the Atlantic seaboard from Bordeaux up to Delfzijl?

When Wilkes was dispatched on the return mission in June 1590, Oldenbarneveldt talked to him as an old friend. He was grateful to the Queen. He was glad to see she meant to reform her army. But he was sorry to hear reports that she thought ill of him, because he was in truth her most devoted servant. And so on. Wilkes cut in to explain that all this was a thing of the past. The sagacious Buckhurst had corrected the Queen's misunderstanding so that she now regarded the Advocate as an instrument of alliance and good will.[21]

The result of Wilkes's mission was to increase mutual confidence. Oldenbarneveldt managed to persuade not only Wilkes but Vere, Norris, Bodley and Gilpin that the Netherlands were no longer a disorganised and headless multitude but a disciplined force firmly under his authority. The Queen might still itch to cut her costs in the Low Countries and get her troops into France. But she found herself contending not only with Oldenbarneveldt's sinuous logic but with Francis Vere's conviction, strengthened by Oldenbarneveldt's persuasive arguments, that the Netherlands were 'the very root' of English strategy. France (said Vere) was only 'the topp branches'.[22] So while the unhappy Bodley, homsesick and seasick, was shuttled to and fro across the North Sea, nagged by the Dutch on one side and lambasted by the Queen on the other,[23] English military strength in the Low Countries remained at its 1585 level until 1598.

Now it was Maurice's turn to break out of the historic redoubt of the north and put Parma's progress into reverse. He began with an uncharacteristically dramatic touch by recapturing Breda, his family seat. The capture of Zutfen, Deventer, Groningen,

Knodsenburg, Arnhem, Hulst and Nijmegen followed with the mechanical precision which placed Maurice in a class apart in that age of casual warfare.[24]

The theory of river defence in its simple form would have surprised him. Zutfen and Deventer were taken from across the river Ysel. Farnese crossed and recrossed the river Waal with large forces. Equally, in the campaign for control of the island of Bommelwaart, between the Maas and the Waal, Maurice and Francis Vere crossed and recrossed the rivers with apparent ease. Late in June 1599 Vere himself slipped an army of six thousand over the Maas. At Nijmegen, in four days, Maurice bridged the Waal with boats, deep and wide though it was, and flung across eight thousand infantry and sixteen companies of cavalry with sixty-eight pieces of heavy artillery. Great morasses were somehow negotiated with heavy siege artillery. Rivers, bogs, marshes he took in his stride.[25]

The basic theory of his military strategy was that the fortified town was vital to offence and defence alike. The capture of Steenwyk in 1592 illustrated his use of the mining engineer and the spade as the army's major brain and weapon. The liberated area expanded steadily till 1597, when his capture of nine strong cities and five great castles finally opened the navigation of the Rhine and secured the eastern bulwark of the Republic. By pushing his frontiers far beyond the so-called river defence line, Maurice had not only securely padlocked the United Provinces; he had also gained control of the trade and navigation of the great rivers themselves. The tide had now turned. So far as England was concerned, the Dutch were no longer suppliants. They were a free and equal partner in the alliance – as long as it lasted.

The costs of the war were enormous. The land operations alone demanded some £600,000 a year, borne in the proportion of 3 to 1 by the Republic and by England. (Even the English share was due to be repaid, and was repaid, when the Treaty of Nonsuch came to an end.) Financial burdens of this order would have been crushing in the days of William the Silent. They were carried now, and buoyantly, because of the enormous and rapid expansion of the Dutch economy. Its core was the trade in corn, iron, tar and naval stores between the Baltic and Gibraltar, and the return trade in salt, herrings and silver. This was the trade which contemporaries described as the 'spine', 'the vital nerve', 'the mother trade' and so on, and it far surpassed in value and strategic importance any other branch of overseas trade.[26] The Dutch grip on this main highway of European trade was ensured by a technological development which did for the Republic something comparable to what steam power was to do for Britain in the nineteenth century. In 1596 the first *fluit* (or 'flyboat', as the English called it) was built at Hoorn. The flyboat was really a sea-going barge. It carried a heavy cargo and it was cheap to build and sail. With its aid the Dutch ran any potential rivals out of the market, especially in corn. And corn was what the world wanted. The population explosion of the sixteenth century had reduced the former food surpluses in the Mediterranean and elsewhere. Everywhere deficits had appeared, not least in England. Swiftly the Dutch entrepreneurs seized their opportunity, trading in grain from the great plains south and east of the Baltic as far south and east as the eastern Mediterranean.[27]

This was, and remained, the basic trade, the source of much of the wealth of Amsterdam, a city now comparable to Antwerp in its greatest days. The nineties and the first two decades of the seventeenth century saw longer trade routes proliferating in the wake of the great pathfinders – Barendz, Heemskerck, Linschoten, Gerrit, Houtman and many others. Dutch traders thrust down to West Africa, the Cape of Good Hope and beyond to India, Ceylon and Java, then to Australia, Tasmania and New Zealand; north to Nova Zembla, Spitsbergen, the Sea of Tartary; across the Atlantic to North America, the Caribbean and down to Cape Horn. Tropical spices, sugar, tobacco, cotton and whale oil joined the flow of traditional products of the Baltic, Biscay and Spanish trades.

The other necessary ingredient in the recipe of economic success was the stream of human emigration from the southern Netherlands. For reasons of faith or convenience, traders and artisans had been trickling away from the Flemish and Walloon provinces ever since Alba's day. They had established the New Draperies in Norwich and Colchester and set up busy workshops with novel crafts throughout the growing London suburbs. Others had taken their skills as silk-weavers, linen-bleachers and worsted-makers to Amsterdam and Haarlem and turned Leyden into the largest cloth-making city in the world. To an important extent the economy of the north was the work of southerners, and their numbers had expanded rapidly after Parma's conquest of Antwerp, Ghent

E 2

and the other great cities of the south had killed the last hopes of achieving a united Netherlands. They now contributed much of the enterprise, technology and knowledge of world markets vital to the economic growth of the north, which was able to take over, as it were, a prefabricated network of markets, trades and industries from the south. The Calvinists and Sephardic Jews of Antwerp brought with them not only uncommon diligence in business but a broad web of commercial contacts which was to help to put Amsterdam on its feet as a world entrepôt.

The loss to the south was incalculable. For more than ten years it had been pillaged and ravaged by bands of mutinous soldiers, Spanish, Flemish, Walloon and German. Its cities were in ruins, its capital and skill were draining away. Most of all, the spirit that had made it the original centre of resistance had evaporated, giving way to apathy and inertia.

When Parma died, he was succeeded by the fat, gouty, melancholy and incompetent Archduke Ernest, brother of the Emperor Rudolph. But not for long. After a year Ernest died and made way for Don Pedro Enriquez, Count of Fuentes, a relative and pupil of Alba and an altogether more formidable character than Ernest. The last degrading farce of the Walloon nobility was now played out. Aerschot, still chief of the magnates, was furiously jealous at Fuentes' appointment. No attempts at comfort by Aremberg (his son-in-law), Chimay (his son) or Havrech (his brother) could pacify him. When they ventured to hint to Philip that 10,000 florins would soothe his tantrums, Fuentes put his foot down. 'Your Majesty knows very well what he is: he is nothing but talk.' So Aerschot retired to Venice, to die there a few months later in December 1595.[28] After more than a quarter of a century the nobility had learned nothing. They still ran true to form, quarrelsome, greedy and intriguing to the last.[29] As Esteban de Ibarra had said, they were a poor lot, weak and unreliable.* Yet for them Spain had spent at the rate of approximately £1¼ million a year between 1567 and 1608 on the Flanders army alone, lost two if not three Armadas, together with the fleet destroyed by Heemskerck at Gibraltar, and sustained the damage of the Anglo-Dutch raids of 1596 on Portugal and Cadiz.† One need seek no more sophisti-

* See pp. 146–7 n. 46.
† Ironically, the Anglo-Dutch raid on Cadiz also resulted in severe losses to the Dutch merchants who owned great stocks there.

cated causes than these to explain the wild inflation, the crazy structure of damaging, crushing taxation and the government bankruptcy that spelt the ultimate material ruin and stagnation of Spain. The net result of Spain's profligate spending of life and money was summed up by Champagny, now doddering, gouty and increasingly eccentric, but still waspishly lucid. The south, he declared, was administered without justice or policy, preyed on, plundered and demoralised. It was empty of trade or hope.[30] Yet his proposed nostrum showed that he too had learned nothing. More priests and monks, he urged, should be injected into this corrupt society and the rules for the confirmation of bishops should be tightened up.

Perhaps it was not altogether strange that Oldenbarneveldt should have felt that the south could still be recovered. The plan to invade Flanders in 1600 was his; its execution fell to Maurice, with Sir Francis Vere leading the first attack on Nieupoort. The first reports seemed to justify all the ebullient optimism of Oldenbarneveldt and evoked sparkling compliments from Elizabeth. But as the facts trickled home, the operation was seen to be a hopeless failure. Oldenbarneveldt's expectations of a rising and a liberation were disappointed. The population were not merely apathetic: they were positively hostile and sick of war. And efficient as Maurice's military revolution was technologically, he had failed to cover one vital aspect of reform: his intelligence system was too poor to tell him anything about southern sentiment or morale. A simultaneous approach from the southern States-General to Oldenbarneveldt similarly came to nothing, in spite of a sumptuous reception provided by Oldenbarneveldt at Bergen-op-Zoom. There proved to be no basis for agreement.[31]

But now the pattern of the war was changing again. To Elizabeth the Netherlands revolt had never been a cause of enthusiasm; at best it had been an unavoidable, at worst a deplorable, drain of money. The danger to Antwerp had trapped her into an apparently endless commitment. Now the star of France had risen. After the miscarriage of a last ill-advised scheme to recover Calais[32] she had entered into a treaty with Henry of Navarre.[33] Burghley was against it but was over-ridden. The Dutch disliked it but were eventually let into it too. It did not last long. By the Treaty of Vervins two years later (May 1598) Henry made his peace with Spain. The steam was fast running out of the war. Europe seemed to be back to Cateau-Cambrésis. There had been a complete change of cast on the political stage. Walsingham, Leicester, Burghley and Norris were all dead. Even Buckhurst was converted to the young Cecil's belief that the Dutch should now make their peace with Spain. Only Essex stood out for continuing the war; and Essex fell from grace in July 1598. Now there was nobody to stop Elizabeth from trying to rid herself of the incubus of Nonsuch. For a year she had been preparing the way, at the same time assuring Caron, the States envoy, that she would have nothing to do with any scheme for returning the United Provinces to Spain. The hope of a financial settlement even sweetened her into one of those almost friendly, if loftily patronising comments with which she was nowadays occasionally pleased to favour her allies. 'It is true', she told Caron, 'that I feel your Government does not always manage things as it should and it does not always treat princes, including myself, as we ought to be treated. But your State is not a Monarchy and we must take everything together and weigh its faults against its many perfections.'[34]

Another series of exhausting journeys to England by Oldenbarneveldt, a few more Queenly tantrums and the business was finally settled. The Queen got her £800,000 – two-thirds of what she claimed under Nonsuch – to be repaid in thirteen yearly instalments. She kept the cautionary towns and a representative on the Council of State. Oldenbarneveldt claimed nevertheless that he had 'conserved Her Majesty's favour and friendship' for his country.[35]

Up to a point it was true. The new Anglo-Dutch arrangements, like Henry's Treaty of Vervins, left it open for the former allies to go on providing troops for the Dutch – so long as the Dutch paid. This put the Queen in an altogether better temper. Vere and his brother continued to command for Maurice. The Duke of Buccleuch, with new reinforcements was sent for the defence of Ostend. The first reports of the battle of Nieupoort had sent the Queen into ecstasies of fulsome praise. 'The sagacious administration of the States Government is so full of good order and policy as far to surpass in its wisdom the intelligence of kings and potentates . . . we kings understand nothing of such affairs in comparison, but require, all of us, to go to school to the States General.'[36] It was vexing, after this moving ceremony of the eating of the words, that the news of a glorious victory turned out to be premature.

When the Queen died, the battle for Ostend was still on; the most bitter, destructive and prolonged of the entire war. Within fourteen days of Elizabeth's death, Oldenbarneveldt was on his way once more with a delegation to present the States-General's compliments to the new King. James, though amiably surprised at the speed of their recognition, and even prepared to help over Ostend, needed no instruction in the sinfulness of rebellion and the undesirability of rebels. The delegation had a cool reception, while James chattered away the hours pouring State secrets into the ears of the Spanish and French Ambassadors. Once more Spanish influence at Court was growing. The ducats (to repeat an earlier observer) were on the trot again, and the Howards, the Nottinghams, the Northamptons, to say nothing of Robert Cecil himself, were agreeably aware of their presence. Cecil's plan was well known. Its attractions increased as faith in a Dutch victory faded and the belief grew – illusory though it was – that the new kings in Spain and their regents in the Netherlands would be less intolerant and oppressive than their predecessors. Essentially, Cecil's plan was inherited directly from his father's of thirty years before: a union of the whole seventeen provinces under the nominal sovereignty of the Archduke. Its chances of success were equally negligible.

On all sides events pointed to a peace, or at least a pause. South of the Scheldt the Dutch had enough strong points to control the traffic on the estuary, but the desolation that was now Ostend finally had to be surrendered to the new Genoese commander, Spinola. The attack reluctantly undertaken by Maurice had revealed the apathy of the south. The French were out of the war. Yet the speed of the Anglo-Spanish peace negotiations surprised Oldenbarneveldt. The negotiators met at Somerset House on 30 May 1604. On 28 August peace was established. The treaty was a rambling, ambiguous affair which gave the cautionary towns to England and left loopholes for 'volunteer' forces to continue help to the Dutch. Oldenbarneveldt remarked to Winwood, Gilpin's successor on the Council of State, 'Litera occidet, spiritus autem vivificat'. But for once even the incorrigible optimist was whistling to keep his courage up. The Dutch had to face the ugly truth that they had now lost all their allies. However unsatisfactory they might have been, their very presence had given diplomatic support to the new state. The names of Yorke, Stanley and Wingfield

might be synonymous with treachery. The Queen's reputation
for reliability might be low. But the support given over the years
by Walsingham, Buckhurst, Rogers, Davison and many others was
well known. The gallantry of Sidney, the Norrises, the Veres, the
Morgans and their fellow-commanders was widely honoured.
Some officers and ranks would fight on, but now they were paid
mercenaries. Politically and militarily, the Republic was on its
own and its prospects of any decisive victory were poor. It was
only a matter of time before the Truce with Spain was signed in
1609.

It lasted twelve years, until 1621, when the Republic was drawn
back into the long-drawn-out complexities of the Thirty Years
War. The years to 1660 were to see some adjustments to the
boundaries of 1609. Maurice's successor, Frederick Henry, was
to make further inroads into the south, capturing Maastricht and
's Hertogenbosch. The 1630s were to revive hopes of a southern
revolt against Spain but, as usual, the southern nobility bungled
their chances and the current Duke of Aerschot found himself
gaoled for life in Madrid, like Montigny and Bergen seventy years
earlier. The south was irrevocably 'espagnolised', bureaucratised,
catholicised. Another segment of the south had to be ceded to
France in 1659. There we leave it and turn to examine the consequences of English policy after 1567.

Conclusion

By English policy we mean the Queen's policy. All those with intimate knowledge who spoke or wrote about the conduct of government business, from Walsingham in the 1570s to Sir Henry Unton (Elizabeth's ambassador to Henry IV in 1596) in the Queen's last years, were emphatically agreed on one point: the Council might propose; the Queen disposed. She might be constrained by circumstances; rarely if ever by people. In so far as personal responsibility can be assigned for the successes or failures of English policy towards the Netherlands in this first and decisive half of the Eighty Years War, the glory or the shame is the Queen's and nobody else's. Professor Hurstfield has asked pertinently, 'Was there a Tudor despotism after all?'[1] It is hard to think of an Elizabethan Privy Councillor who would not have returned a heartfelt affirmation, certainly where foreign policy was concerned.[2]

A second point. In trying to assess the consequences of Queen Elizabeth, we have to steer a difficult course between underestimating her difficulties and overestimating her personal achievements. Sentiment and hind sight make the second temptingly attractive. Did not England survive and up to a point prosper? Did not the Dutch Republic do likewise? Did not Spain start on the downward path? Was not France rescued from half a century of civil war and chaos? Was not all this, then, in some measure the Queen's doing, and did not the prevarications and subterfuges in reality conceal the masterly pursuit of well-defined ends by a diplomat and strategist of genius?[3]

In trying to answer such questions we must not lose sight of the duty which Elizabeth was there to fulfil: the defence of the realm of England. Sentiment for or against the Dutch, antipathy to the King of Spain or sympathy for the condition of France were factors she had to weigh in their context simply as part of England's problem of security and well-being. We cannot deal in hypothetical solutions to these problems which were not available to the Queen or her Council at the time. We can only deal in the courses open to her, considered by her and recommended to her, in the light of information known to be available to her and to her advisers.

Let us first remind ourselves of the basic facts. Before the Revolt the seventeen Netherlands provinces that came into the hands of Charles V had formed something of a cultural unity, even the rudiments of political unity, even though their inhabitants spoke four different tongues – Dutch, Low German, Frisian and French. The Revolt itself was for a time a revolt of the whole of these Netherlands provinces. The suggestion made earlier in these lectures was that the withdrawal of what are now Belgium, Luxembourg and Artois (the return of the first two to obedience to Spain and the cession of Artois to France) cannot be wholly explained by simple theories of the indefensible nature of their terrain. By 1609 the Netherlands were irrevocably divided, and we need to invoke politics as well as strategy, tactics and topography to explain how a society once one of the wealthiest, most powerful and most virile in Europe simply disappeared from sight, to become a mere remnant of old Burgundy doomed to suffer enslavement successively to Spain, Austria, Holland, Germany and finally to its own internal dissensions.[4]

Dr Rowse has presented an optimistic view of the 'Obedient Provinces' turning into a 'virtually independent' power, delivered out of the hands of France while 'the Netherlands as a unity came into the possession of no great power'.[5] Geyl's alternative interpretation – a remnant of southern provinces who 'were no longer masters of their souls' – seems to me nearer the truth. It is upon this truly tragic view of Belgian history that my remarks here are based.

Strategically, the existence of this political vacuum was a standing invitation to a resurgent France to invade and expand after 1660. Spain now being reduced to impotence, it fell to England and the Dutch Republic, indeed in the end to all the great powers, Protestant and Catholic, to keep France out of the southern Netherlands. After 1715 they were tossed into the lap of Austria, which would have preferred to take Bavaria. Down to the mid-eighteenth century they were defended, theoretically, by a barrier of fortresses manned by the Dutch. But the system provided no real defence against France and by the mid-century this Maginot Line of barrier fortresses was in ruins. The rest of the century saw the entire Netherlands pass steadily into the orbit of France. Not only Marlborough's wars but Wellington's too were a consequence of the late-sixteenth-century division of the Netherlands.

For all the burgeoning of Dutch wealth and power in the seventeenth century, the seven United Provinces were too small to carry indefinitely the insupportable burden of military and naval defence they had to bear.[6]

If the Burgundian possessions could have been preserved intact (and expanded eastwards to the Rhine, as they might well have been), it would have been a different story. But by 1648 all hopes of a reunification had gone. Powerfully entrenched interests in Holland were now jealous of 'Belgian' independence because of the potential rivalry it threatened from Antwerp. England herself was now jealous lest the Dutch, whom she had now come to regard as commercial rivals, should acquire more power in the south. The south itself was unready and unwilling to face independence. The Belgian people, as Geyl says, were simply submerged.[7] For one reason or another, a potentially powerful nation-state had been disrupted, fragmented and lost to view.

Professor Wernham has explained, and gallantly defended, Elizabeth's foreign policy towards the Netherlands in a number of penetrating and persuasive essays.[8] His main argument can be summarised in the following passage: 'The aim [of Elizabeth's policy towards the Netherlands Revolt], put quite simply, was to get the Spanish army out of the Netherlands without letting the French in.'[9] This policy was decided by considerations of national defence, by fear of France as much as by fear of Spain. It meant 'persuading Philip II to withdraw his foreign forces'. It meant ensuring they did not return. This could best be done by restoring to the Netherlands their ancient liberties but not granting them their independence. The 'nominal sovereignty' of Spain was essential (it is argued) to preserve them from attack by France. Between 1572 and 1578 this policy 'came very near to success' because France was too weak and divided to interfere in the Netherlands. Then the French began to meddle again, in the person of Anjou. There followed the split of 1579 into the Arras and Utrecht Unions and the arrival of Parma. Yet, says Professor Wernham, Elizabeth's policy 'remained intelligible until 1585'. (One can agree that, intelligible or not, Robert Cecil and James I were still clinging to it nearly twenty years later.)

There seem to me to be serious difficulties in accepting this argument or the variants upon it elaborated elsewhere. If its aim was to get the Spanish army out of the Netherlands, it was a hopeless failure. The Spanish army departed for a short period only after 1576 because it was chaotically fragmented and demoralised by mutiny. But from 1567 to 1576 it had been there, in spite of all Netherlands protests, and it returned again in 1582, to remain indefinitely in the southern provinces, and in the eastern provinces until it was driven out by Maurice. No mention is made of the degree of responsibility which many contemporaries, including William the Silent himself, Walsingham, Leicester, Wilson, Davison and many others believed Elizabeth bore for the schism which developed between the Walloons and the rest between 1577 and 1579: and how this schism led directly to the permanent division of north and south. But to that I will return in a moment.

We have followed the laborious repetitions by Burghley of the plea to Spain to restore the Netherlands' ancient liberties. We have noted the resounding silence with which these appeals were received. It is difficult to believe that Elizabeth, in many respects such a political realist, regarded them as anything more than a conveniently empty formula which could be drawn upon and repeated without commitment or expense, enabling her to enjoy a reputation for statesmanship and perhaps for humanity as well. For it was one thing to parley with Alba, Requesens or Parma. Some concessions might seem to be made by these local commanders. But she knew only too well that any concessions or compromises would be consigned to the waste-paper basket as soon as they reached the Escorial.[10] To talk of the 'rights' of Protestants or dissident subjects to Philip was like talking to Hitler of the 'rights' of the Jews or to the Kremlin of the 'rights' of Czechs, Poles or Hungarians. But could the devious, indecisive ponderings of Elizabeth and Burghley all have been an ingeniously calculated part of a farseeing diplomatic game? If so, what were the other motives that justified policies which must threaten, sooner or later, the security of England and the life of the Queen? How far, for example, was the fear of France, of which the Queen made so much, justified?

Elizabeth's policy towards France is even less easy to elucidate than her policy towards Philip, who was theoretically at any rate the legatee of the Burgundian tradition. That her fear of France was genuine is just as certain as that it was (in the short term at least) exaggerated, for virtually from her accession onwards, France was racked by one civil war after another. As Professor

Wernham has remarked, even Henry IV's conversion to Catholicism in 1593 did not mean the full recovery of France.[11] Nearly half a century more was to pass before the French threat to the Spanish Netherlands was to become serious. It was certainly fear of French influence which had driven her covertly to send a handful of troops to Flushing in 1572. Yet in the same year she cheerfully signed the Treaty of Blois with France! By 1581–2 her repeated failures to fulfil her promise of effective military help to the Netherlands were a major, probably the major, factor which drove them into the arms of the French in the shape – the very unpleasing shape – of Anjou. Hence the next and lowest ebb of absurdity, the Anjou marriage proposal, which carried with it the Queen's support for jobbing him into the position as sovereign of the Netherlands.[12]

By this time William had no alternative but to acquiesce in a policy for which he has been criticised as pro-French.[13] He was likewise driven into the equally deplorable necessity to employ Duke Casimir as a counterweight to this French influence in the south. For Casimir's first – and indeed almost his only – action was to encourage those very Calvinist fanatics who, along with the Paternoster Jacks on the opposing side, did more than anybody to kill the hopes of the Queen and of William the Silent of a united Netherlands. Casimir's follies at Ghent led straight to the Catholic Union of Arras. Simultaneously the northern provinces, still cold-shouldered and disappointed by England, turned more and more to France. William assassinated, the Queen snatched momentarily at the idea of a joint Anglo-French protectorate of the Low Countries, only to retreat as she contemplated the alternative threats from France and Spain. She could no longer avoid military intervention. She only managed to delay it long enough to help to lose Antwerp, the key to the south.

Elizabeth's fear of France, like her reverence for Spain, was rooted more in superstition than in reason. Obstinate, obsessive conservatism was also the key to her attitude to the Netherlands. The Netherlanders were first and foremost rebels. Elizabeth Tudor was heir to an England still deeply divided. She was no less heir to that traumatic horror of civil war and rebellion which was the legacy of the Wars of the Roses.[14] The idea of rebellion upset all her fundamental notions of the universal order of things, bringing her face to face with novel political situations she abominated and feared. If the rebels were heretics too, that only made it worse. They also threatened to cost her money, a great deal of money. As Farnese, among many others, had observed, the Queen was a woman and 'by no means fond of expense'.[15] Above all, so far as the Dutch were concerned, she was a snob. How much more agreeable and rewarding to chatter with the Marquis of Havrech or dance with the smooth and courtly Champagny than to argue with these upstart merchants from the waterside and warehouses of Scheldt and Maas! What possible hope of success could be entertained for this headless motley of corn and tallow chandlers, sawyers, salters and fishermen, pitted as they were against the best army of Europe, led by the cream of its nobility?

However the fortunes of the rebels moved, it was difficult for them to win in the battle of wits with the Queen. Never one to back a losing horse deliberately, she turned away from them when they seemed to be losing. When things went better, she would warm a little towards them. But if they showed signs of winning, this was a perfect reason for not wasting her (admittedly) very limited resources. To this diplomatic coquetry the Dutch had their own reply. When they stuck to the letter of their instructions and declined to be bullied into agreements without reference home, the Queen took it for mere contumacy.

The cauldron boiled over on a wintry day late in January 1587 at Greenwich. After reproaching the five visiting Dutch envoys for a variety of crimes and follies, she switched abruptly to problems of status and polity. Princes, she informed them loftily, 'transact business in a certain way and with a princely intelligence such as private persons cannot imitate'. The visitors might be 'chieftains' but in regard to Princes they were merely individuals. 'Among us Princes we are not wont to make such long orations as you do, but you ought to be content with the few words we bestow upon you and make yourself quiet thereby.' In future she would be treated more honourably. She would appoint 'some personages' from her Council to deal with the Dutch instead of meeting them herself. And so she swept from the apartment.[16]

Conservatism, parsimony, snobbery, distrust: these explain her refusal to commit herself down to 1585. By then it was too late to save the unity of the Netherlands. Her attitude to the Dutch changed only as their successes in the nineties proved even to the Queen that she had miscalculated their capacity not only to survive but to prosper. The Treaty of Nonsuch had pitched her into heavy expenses which (as Philip Sidney observed) might have been avoided if she had listened to her advisers earlier; and this at a time when the national finances were less able to bear them.[17] No one will be found to argue that Leicester's escapades from 1586 to 1587 were anything but politically and militarily discreditable and damaging. Neither Sir John Neale nor Professor Wernham defends him. As for the Queen, Professor Wernham's verdict is that 'it was not the Queen's policy that was at fault. It was her inability to control its instruments.'[18] Both exonerate the Queen at Leicester's expense. But, even granted that it was difficult to control commanders and armies overseas in the sixteenth century, can it be seriously maintained that the Queen's handling of Leicester showed any greater wisdom than Leicester's handling of his Dutch allies? Or the appointment of Yorke and Stanley? Or the whole disastrous strategy of the expedition? The choice of Leicester was an error of the first magnitude. It can be explained but not excused by the Queen's personal attachment to her 'Sweet Robin' and by her hope that he was rich enough to dig into his own capacious pocket and save her money. Her conduct of the whole episode seems to me hysterical and confused.

Yet the real gravamen of the charge against the Queen does not relate to the Leicester period, gross though the mismanagement of it was. By then she had at least taken a decision which helped substantially to preserve the independence of the northern provinces. The worst damage was inflicted between 1575 and 1579 (and perhaps 1585), when the prospect of a united Netherlands still beckoned. It was the view of a majority of her ministers throughout those years, and during at least three crises the unanimous view of all the ministers concerned (including even Burghley), that it was urgently necessary to send immediate and effective aid to the Netherlands. The Queen herself accepted this policy. She professed to regard William as the only salvation of the Netherlands and implicitly accepted his argument (always shared by many of her advisers and more than once by all) that the security and prosperity of England was indissolubly bound with that of a united Netherlands. Yet on each occasion when the moment of decision arrived, she suffered one of her characteristic last-minute blackouts. The onlooker is irresistibly reminded of Churchill's attack on the Baldwin Government three and a half centuries later: 'So they go on in strange paradox, decided only to be undecided, resolved to be irresolute, adamant for drift, solid for fluidity, all powerful to be impotent.'[19]

The Queen's foreign and military policy was her own. The principles were rooted deep in her psychology, her intuitions and her heritage. But the execution and application of the principles she left to others. It was, above all, Burghley – her 'Spirit' – who turned the principles into formulae. The partnership has often been regarded as undoubtedly a fortunate one for England. This view seems to me too simple. The qualities that made Burghley an outstanding royal servant in domestic affairs – the combination of Welsh and Midlands country cunning, the legal acumen, the administrative flair – were of less value in the maze of European diplomacy than they were in negotiating the religious settlement, dealing with economic policy or home security. To Burghley, Europe was a continent almost as strange as the Indies or the Americas, whose topography and denizens he could only know from their representations in his great collection of maps and pictures. Foreign travel he cordially disliked and he did not renew his brief and superficial acquaintance with the Continent made in Mary's time. To the 'Manor of England' he devoted a stewardship as faithful and laborious as that by which he concurrently aggregated the Cecil dynastic establishment – the great mansions and estates at Theobalds and Cheshunt Park, Burghley House by Stamford, Cecil House in the Strand – replete with a pedigree which converted the modest Monmouth family of *Sitsilt* into a branch of the Roman *Caecilii* (not without a few sniggers behind the hand from the sceptics).[20]

Diplomatically, Burghley floundered in the wake of his mistress's obsessions, doing his best to convert prejudices into policies, usually deferential to her dominant will and only deviating when it seemed that they were both confronted by Nemesis or a unanimity of opposition amongst the Queen's other counsellors. Nevertheless the errors were prolonged and serious. The formula by which he purported to preserve the Netherlands' liberties without upsetting Spain quickly became not only meaningless but dangerous to England's own security. Until 1585, in spite of three or four spasmodic frights at the Spanish or French menace, nothing was done. Antwerp was lost. Then Leicester was let loose.

Until the Armada was approaching the shores of England, Burghley allowed quite irresponsible negotiations with Parma, transacted through two ridiculous Genoese–Antwerper merchants, Grafigny and van Loo, to drift on, with great damage to England's relations with her Netherlands ally by treaty.[21] The disastrous Portugal and Islands voyages were similarly encouraged. When he finally came round to the view that it was, after all, a threat to the security of England to dally with Spain any longer, his remedy was the Anglo-French *entente* of the 1590s: a medicine (as things were to prove) worse than the disease.

Walsingham, in character and convictions, stood in strong contrast to the Lord Treasurer. Burghley's weakness was Walsingham's strength. Mary's reign he had spent travelling on the Continent, gaining an intimate knowledge of people and affairs in Geneva, France and the Low Countries. From 1570 until his appointment as one of the Queen's principal Secretaries of State in 1573 he was resident Ambassador in Paris, where he widened still further his already extensive network of acquaintances in Europe. His own keen powers of observation and the reports of the efficient espionage network he maintained throughout Europe led him to the conviction that England's peril lay in a dominant Spain; her security in a free Netherlands. Where Burghley was so often sententious, prolix and hesitant, Walsingham was incisive, clear and sharp. His convictions were never weakened or compromised and as occasion demanded he put them squarely to the Queen. This did not endear him to her and more than once she accused him, but without conviction, of disloyalty to her person. Her relations with him were nevertheless inevitably affected. She disliked his opinions, which pointed to a sympathy for rebellion and a tendency to support it by financial imprudence.

Walsingham never enjoyed the influence wielded by the more malleable Burghley, and his disregard for his personal welfare left him a relatively poor man, enjoining upon his executors at his death in 1590 an austerity funeral for the sake of his creditors. How different from the Cecil affluence! Yet much of our Tudor historiography mirrors the Queen's partiality for Burghley, even though he was proved dismally wrong in his policies and predictions regarding foreign affairs, while Walsingham's distrust of Spain and understanding of the Dutch role in the defence of England were amply borne out by events.

If any statesman deserved an Anglo-Dutch memorial it was Walsingham. Yet his loyalty and his judgement were scurvily rewarded. The Queen's most recent biographer has summarised a generation of Tudor historiography. Of the Queen's last, darkening years he has written: 'The great men of her age were leaving her. Some she could spare without a pang, like Walsingham, the pale Puritan. . . .'[22] But was it his Puritanism she hated, or the fact that he was, alone among her counsellors, the one who consistently and fearlessly told her the unpalatable truth?

For although he was a strong supporter of overseas expansion and maritime power, Walsingham never pretended that England could abandon her involvement in Europe. To try and retain Calais was futile, but the presence of a friendly power further north along the western seaboard of the Continent was as vital to England's security as it had been in the full flush of the Burgundian alliance. To see Spain in this role as the natural successor to Burgundy (as Burghley and the Queen wanted to do) was to practise mere self-deception. The idea of an alternative defence policy based on Atlantic expansion, or a maritime ascendancy severed from a sound strategic position *vis-à-vis* the continental seaboard was likewise a delusion. There was a tough realism about Walsingham's mind that saved him from slipping into the romantic dream-world that was often to seduce more gullible men. The need to preserve the Low Countries in reliable hands might be expensive and exasperating but it could not be dodged. As Professor Elton has written: 'the primacy of a global and oceanic role has never been as noticeable in the day-to-day labours of the policy-makers, as it is in the writings of propagandists or the reflections of historians.'[23] It was not so much that the Queen and Burghley were consciously removing their diplomatic and strategic centre of gravity out of continental Europe as that they were trying to shut their eyes to the costs and consequences of the need for it to stay there.

The Queen's preference for Burghley's advice over Walsingham's was not the least of the forces which drove William into the arms of the French. Without her firm financial, military and moral support he could not exert his potential authority over the factious, quarrelsome but influential Walloon nobility. It may be objected that there was no hope of preserving the unity of a society so divided by religion and language. Recent studies of the Revolt do not support this view. They have stressed (as Buckhurst did) the political importance of the large, floating, uncommitted proportion of the population in an age when, as a Dutch authority on the Revolt has reminded us, boundaries of religion were vague and 'the choice of religion determined by all kinds of worldly reasons'.[24] Nor could linguistic differences exercise in that age the divisive, emotive, political and social influences they have developed in more technical and literate societies in more recent times.

If it is objected that this argument exaggerates the potential influence Elizabeth could wield in Netherlands affairs, the answer lies in later events; in the desperate Orange negotiations of 1640–1 for the marriage settlement that linked the houses of Orange and Stuart in the persons of the Stadholder Frederick Henry's son William (later William II) and Charles I's daughter Mary. Long after the Stuart cause was seen to be lost, the Orange party and their Calvinist support hung on doggedly to the Stuart alliance Why? Because of the prestige and power a monarchical link was thought to give to a pseudo-dynasty which knew that its own origins were rooted in rebellion. Elizabeth, so sensitive herself to the divinity that could hedge a king, was singularly blind to its potency where the Croys, Lannoys, Lalaings, Montmorencis and the rest of the Netherlands nobility were concerned. It is supremely ironical that one so convinced of the power of kingship at home should have failed so disastrously to measure its ability to succour an ally abroad.[25]

The polarisation into north and south, Protestant and Catholic, was only beginning in the 1570s. William still had numerous relatives and allies among the Walloon nobility. Long after his own conversion to Protestantism, Aerschot, Lalaing, Havrech, Hèze, Glymes, Chimay, Rennenberg, van den Bergh, Hoogstraten, even Champagny, and many others promised him their support in working for a united Netherlands. They defected, as William warned Elizabeth they would, because he could get no firm support from her (though she was perfectly prepared to upbraid them for deserting him). At no time did the Queen or any of her advisers (except Buckhurst) show any sign of understanding the nature of the Erasmian, moderate Protestantism which was the religion most favoured by the merchant rulers of the cities. This remained as elusive a mystery to the English as the Anglican Settlement was (and still is) to the Netherlanders. There were few more perverse twists to Elizabeth's foreign policy than its rejection of the moderates and its spasmodic encouragement of the very fanatics whom the Queen detested most cordially at home. On this Casimir and Leicester were disastrously at one.[26] Thus the chance of a Third Force on the European continent was lost for ever.

Again it may be argued that such a power would have threatened England: perhaps, but this was certainly not the reason for Elizabeth's prevarication. On the contrary; steeped as she was in traditions of monarchical authority, she could no more comprehend how a constitution without a divinely ordained head could possibly work than she could comprehend how a Netherlands economy innocent of governmental *dirigisme* and a Netherlands society without a ruling aristocracy could survive, let alone expand and prosper.[27] Her policy, or lack of it, contributed to the disintegration of that society, to the drift first of both north and south towards France, then of the south back to Spain. Without the seduction of the Walloon nobility by Parma, the great Spanish enterprise against England would have been impossible. Assured of their support and deploying the newly recalled Spanish army, Parma was far stronger than any of his predecessors had been. The truth of William's reiterated conviction was now inescapable. The threat to the Netherlands and the threat to England were inseparably connected, two halves of a single strategy.

The argument that she was short of money, that the demands of home defence, Ireland especially, had to be first priority, is cogent. No critic can deny that the Queen faced fearsome difficulties political and financial. Yet again, we must recall that not only William the Silent but her own councillors, commanders and Members of Parliament repeatedly tried to make her see that sooner or later she would have to pay the bill for the defence of her realm against Spain;* that the Netherlands in Spanish hands were no less a threat to England than an occupied Ireland.[28]

All her six Parliaments after 1585 granted her subsidies. Some were positively embarrassing in their desire to finance even more amply the vigorous pursuit of the Netherlands campaign. In 1586–1587 she refused Parliament's offer of benevolences. Sir John Neale has explained that this was because she was determined not to be beholden to Parliament. True, but this is different from arguing that her dislike of the war arose from unavoidable poverty.[29]

* See p. 95 (Sidney), and pp. 34, 55–6, 60–1 (William).

The argument that even if finance had been adequate it was difficult to turn money into an effective military force, properly armed and led, is also important.[30] Yet it can be overstated. The Netherlands cause drew enthusiastic popular support from all classes of Englishmen and it does not seem to have been difficult to obtain soldiers. The difficulty was to keep them under arms. 'The flower', lamented the Mustermaster-general Digges, illegally bought themselves out of service by 'thirty or forty pounds a-piece' with which they crossed their officers' palms. In their place came 'paddy persons', which helps to account for the large number of those Irish kerns whose appearance and indiscipline caused general alarm.[31] These were additional to the thousands of mercenaries recruited for service with the States-General. To provide officers and administrators was a more serious problem, but the skirmishes of 1572–3 had revealed the talents of leaders later to be famous, like Thomas Morgan and Roger Williams. At the victory of Rijmenant (1577) John Norris had demonstrated brilliantly what his English and Scots volunteers were capable of. The campaigns after 1588 showed that all that was needed to produce a seasoned corps of officers was practice and experience. Again, we must ask whether it was the resources or the will that was lacking to the Queen.[32]

Nor does it hold water to argue in favour of Elizabeth's persistent canvassing for continued Spanish sovereignty that when the Netherlands were in the fullness of time legally recognised as free and independent, their reward was to be exposed to the threat of France at a time when Spain had become too weak to defend Belgium.[33] For by then the European situation was entirely transformed. The Netherlands had been divided for a century, the south totally demoralised; the north was already groaning under its burden of defence costs, and France had risen to a European hegemony which Elizabeth's support for Henry IV had itself helped to make possible.[34] Burghley's accusation, quoted earlier in these lectures, went to the root of the matter. The Dutch also were only too conscious that where the Spanish foot trod, no grass grew. It remained the conviction underlying the *Maxims* of Johan de Witt nearly a century later; the dynastic ambitions of a centralised monarchy were totally incompatible with the prosperity, even the survival, of a society and economy based on international trade, as that of the Republic was. Spanish sovereignty was not an umbilical cord: it was a strangler's rope.

It is more than usually difficult to separate Elizabeth's private motives and actions from the tangle of public affairs with which they were so closely interwoven. Her personal brilliance dazzled her age, her admirers and her critics, as it still dazzles later ages and historians. We so often encounter that Queen 'of unswerving purpose who could and did stand firm on matters of principle'[35] that her great qualities conceal the weaknesses which often bedevilled her diplomacy and strategy. Few great political leaders have had an equally strong grasp of domestic and foreign affairs, of the problems of peace and war. Elizabeth was no exception. 'She was not', Professor Wernham confesses, 'one of England's great war leaders and she only half achieved her object.'[36] Where I differ from him is that I would extend his verdict to her actions in that sphere of diplomacy which in her times lay half-way between hot war and cold war. Nearly three-quarters of a century ago the admirable Bishop Creighton shrewdly put his finger on the cause of her failures. 'Elizabeth', he wrote, 'had no enthusiasm for a great cause . . . she provided for the present and left the future to care for itself . . . the revolt of the Netherlands supplied another piece which she could play in her cautious game. She felt justified in playing it as it suited her own purposes.'[37] Compare that with Sir Walter Raleigh's famous dictum; 'Her Majesty did all by halves.'[38] So far as the Revolt of the Netherlands is concerned, Raleigh has written the most precise epitaph on Queen Elizabeth's policy. She had indeed helped – in the end – to preserve half the Netherlands, but at the cost of helping to sever and sacrifice the rest.

Notes

ABBREVIATIONS

CSP   Calendar of State Papers
H.M.C. Historical Manuscripts Commission
K   Relations politiques des Pays-Bas et de l'Angleterre, ed. J.
        Kervyn de Lettenhove, 11 vols (Brussels, 1882–1900)

Prelude

1. For recent discussion of the major issues of the Revolt, see G. N.
Clark, 'The Birth of the Dutch Republic', *Proceedings of the British
Academy*, XXXII (1946); Pieter Geyl, *The Revolt of the Netherlands* (3rd
imp., 1958); G. J. Renier, *The Criterion of Dutch Nationhood* (1946);
Britain and the Netherlands, ed. J. S. Bromley and E. H. Kossmann
(1960); *Algemene Geschiedenis der Nederlanden*, IV and V (1952); *The Age
of Expansion*, ed. H. R. Trevor-Roper (1968), esp. ch. III ('The Divided
Netherlands', by Charles Wilson).

2. Like almost everything else about the Revolt, the term 'seventeen
provinces' is controversial. Were there 'seventeen'? Or was 'seventeen'
only a usage to denote a sizeable but indeterminate number of provinces?
For discussion of the historiography of the problem, see Jhr Dr P. J. van
Winter, *Verkenning en Onderzoek* (1965) pp. 82–104.

Chapter 1

1. J. E. Neale, *Elizabeth and Her Parliaments 1581–1601* (1957) pt II,
ch. IV *passim*, quoting Throckmorton's speech, preserved in the Pierpoint
Morgan Library, New York, MS. MA. 276, ff. 28–51. Only three of his
Parliamentary speeches are recorded. Throckmorton, a fire-eater, was
later associated, probably correctly, with the Martin Marprelate tracts.

2. 'In Search of the Queen' by C. H. Williams, in *Elizabethan Government and Society: Essays Presented to Sir John Neale*, ed. Bindoff *et al.*
(1961).

3. Especially, e.g. the (unpublished) thesis of Mr N. G. Parker
(Christ's College, Cambridge) on 'The Spanish Road and the Army of
Flanders 1567–1647', and that of Mr A. W. Lovett (Sidney Sussex College)
on Don 'Luis de Requesens and the Netherlands 1573-1576'. Both are dated
1968.

4. J. W. Smit, 'The Present Position of Studies regarding the Revolt
of the Netherlands', in *Britain and the Netherlands*, ed. Bromley and
Kossmann.

5. R. B. Wernham, 'English Policy and the Revolt of the Nethelands',
ibid.

6. R. B. Wernham, in *Elizabethan Government and Society*, ed. Bindoff
et al., p. 368.

7. B. W. Beckingsale, *Elizabeth I* (1963) pp. 87 and 144. Mr Andrews generally accepts the same thesis, adding that after the Armada she had time on her side: K. R. Andrews, *Elizabethan Privateering* (1964) pp. 7–10.

8. P. Geyl, *Geschiedenis van de Nederlandsche Stam*, 1 (Amsterdam, 1931); translated into English as *The Revolt of the Netherlands 1555–1609* (1932).

9. Both Geyl and Dr A. L. Rowse are wrong in castigating Motley as a 'New England Presbyterian' (Geyl, *The Revolt of the Netherlands*, p. 16) and a 'New England Puritan' (Rowse, *The Expansion of Elizabethan England* (1955) p. 378, n. 1). Motley was a liberal humanist. He was not anti-English. Some of his closest friends were English. He loved London and is buried in Kensal Green Cemetery.

10. *John Lothrop Motley: A Memoir*, by Oliver Wendell Holmes (1878) p. 207. J. L. Motley, *Correspondence*, 1 210–12; Groen van Prinsterer, *Prolégomènes* to his edition of *Archives ou correspondance inédite de la Maison d'Orange Nassau* (1835–47), also his *Handboek der Geschiedenis van het Vaderland* (1846). Bakhuizen's views are presented in his *Studiën en Schetsen over Vaderlandsche Geschiedenis*, 1–v (Amsterdam and The Hague, 1863–1913).

11. S. Muller, *Schetsen uit de Middeleeuwen* (1914) pp. 369–78; G. M. Asher, *Bibliographical and Historical Essays etc.* (1867). Also the discussion by W. J. van Hoboken in *Britain and the Netherlands*, ed. Bromley and Kossmann (1960) 43–5.

12. J. A. van Houtte, *Economische en Sociale Geschiedenis van de Lage Landen* (1964) pp. 205–8.

13. Yet in the most recent survey of the historiography Fruin is himself talked of as muddle-headed. See Smit, in *Britain and the Netherlands*, ed. Bromley and Kossmann, ch. 1; Geyl, *The Revolt of the Netherlands*, pp. 15–18, 258.

14. *The Revolt of the Netherlands*, the *History of the Low Countries* (Trevelyan Lectures, 1964) and *Debates with Historians* (1962) alone contain more than twenty such statements.

15. J. F. Niermeyer in an article on 'The Netherlands' in *Chambers's Encyclopaedia* (1950).

16. See especially *History of the Low Countries* and *Debates with Historians*.

17. C. R. Markham, *The Fighting Veres* (1888) chs IX and X. See also Edward Grimston's *History of the Netherlands* (1627). This is a full account of the strategy and tactics of the Netherlands actions, incorporating a translation of the work of Jean François le Petit, and extracts from the diaries of Roger Williams, an eye-witness of many of the principal battles.

18. E.g. *Debates with Historians*, pp. 216–17.

19. Two more recent commentaries on the Revolt seem equally to neglect or at least to underestimate the effects of external events on its course. G. Griffiths, 'The Revolutionary Character of the Revolt of the Netherlands', in *Comparative Studies in Society and History*, II (1960) can be compared with a Marxist interpretation of the same date, Tibor

Wittman's *Les Gueux dans les 'Bonnes Villes' de Flandre 1577–1584* (Budapest, 1969 but apparently complete by 1961). Although both are perceptive studies of the local, social elements in the Revolt, neither seems to me to pay sufficient attention to the wider context of international events without which the course of affairs cannot be understood. It is this point on which Sir George Clark rightly insists in his Raleigh Lecture (British Academy, 1946) on *The Birth of the Dutch Republic*.

20. The title-page of his *Apologie* (Leyden, 1581) gives him thirteen major titles, along with other etceteras and his offices of state.

21. G. Mattingley, *Renaissance Diplomacy* (1955) p. 87.

22. Ibid.

23. K 1 cclxxxi 393, Wotton to Cecil from Brussels, 9 Jan 1559. See below, pp. 21–2, for the Cateau-Cambrésis negotiations.

24. Bindoff, 'The Greatness of Antwerp', *New Cambridge Modern History*, II; O. de Smedt, *De Engelse Natie te Antwerpen in het 16e. Eeuw.* (Antwerp, 1950) pp. 257 f.; F. J. Fisher, 'Commercial Trends and Policy in 16th-century England', in *Economic History Essays*, ed. E. Carus Wilson (1954).

25. De Smedt, *De Engelse Natie te Antwerpen*, p. 317.

26. R. B. Outhwaite, 'The Trials of Foreign Borrowing', *Economic History Review*, XIX 3 (Aug 1966).

27. R. de Roover, *Gresham on Foreign Exchange*.

28. See J. U. Nef, *The Rise of the British Coal Industry* (1932) I 142 f. Deposits of other ores were exploited but the role of mineral wealth in the English crown economy was never comparable with that in contemporary royal economies abroad.

29. For English figures, see the summary of recent opinion in W. K. Jordan, *Philanthropy in England in 1485–1660* (1959) pp. 25–9. For the Netherlands, see Prof. K. Helleiner in the *Cambridge Economic History of Europe*, IV, ch. I, where it is estimated that Holland doubled its population in the sixteenth century. Prof. J. van Houtte gives figures for the whole Netherlands in 1525 of 1·85 million (by the late eighteenth century the total for the north, south and the bishopric of Liége seems to have been between 4½ to 5 million): *Economische en Sociale Geschiedenis van de Lage Landen*, pp. 131, 204–8. Pirenne thought that the total population of the seventeen provinces in the 1560s was about 3 million. A more recent estimate puts the total at a lower figure of 2 million, of which over half lived in the southern provinces (C. Verlinden, J. Craeybeckx and E. Scholliers, in *Annales: Économies, Sociétés, Civilisations* 10 (1955) 173–98). The problem is complicated by emigration from south to north, by depopulation in the south and growth in the north. A figure of 3 million for the whole area by 1600 does not seem unlikely. Professor Elton has suggested that the seventeen provinces contained a population larger than that of England but gives no date for his surmise (*England under the Tudors* (1955) ch. XIII).

30. *Dutch Drawn to the Life* (1664) p. 42. But for a somewhat different view, see F. Snapper, *Oorlogs invloeden op de Overzeese Handel van Holland 1551–1719* (Amsterdam, 1959), esp. chs I and II and pp. 285–92.

31. Introduction to R. Fruin, *The Siege and Relief of Leyden in 1574* (1924).

32. *Hamlet*, v ii.

Chapter 2

1. *CSP (Foreign)*, 1558–9, no. 422, Mason's report to Cecil from Cateau-Cambrésis, 18 Mar 1559.

2. K i 290.

3. K i 572–612.

4. K ii 91.

5. K ii 206, 332, 413, 569.

6. De Smedt, *De Engelse Natie te Antwerpen*, pp. 340–1.

7. Ibid.

8. See *CSP (Foreign)*, 1566-8: 1964, 26 Jan 1568; 2205, 18 May 1568.

9. See Conyers Read, 'Elizabeth and Alva's Pay Ships', *Journal of Modern History* (1933); R. B. Wernham, *Before the Armada* (1966) pp. 296 ff.; J. B. Black, *The Reign of Elizabeth*, 2nd ed. (1959) pp. 128–34.

10. F. C. Dietz, *English Public Finance 1485–1641* (1964) ii 15, 16. Fisher's article quoted above in *Economic History Essays*, ed. Carus Wilson.

11. George Unwin, *Studies in Economic History* (1927) p. 177. For an equally critical view, see W. R. Scott, *Joint Stock Companies* (1910–12) i 49–52. Unwin compares the boastings of contemporary chroniclers with the ethos of 'the modern yellow Press'.

12. I am indebted to Mr Philip Grierson and Dr Geoffrey Parker of Christ's College, Cambridge, for information on these costs. Dr Parker's estimates are based on his examination of the accounts of the Army Paymasters now conserved in the Archives at Simancas. I have converted the escudo (or 'single pistolate') at the rate of 5/10*d* to the pound sterling. (R. Recorde, *Grounde of Artes* (1582).)

13. For contemporary descriptions of the loss, see Bernardino de Mendoza, *Comentarios de las guerras de los Páises Bajos*, v 10 (Biblioteca de Autores Españoles, Tomo 28, Madrid, 1948). Mendoza was an officer with Alba at this time. Later he became Ambassador to England.

14. *Les Gueux de Mer*, by Roger Avermaete (Brussels, 1944) gives the best recent account, especially chs iii–viii.

15. See the article by J. K. Oudendijk in *Bijdragen voor de Geschiedenis de Nederlanden* (1964). He took his share of their profitable raids on enemy shipping, which his sanction promoted from piracy into privateering. As allies the Beggars were disreputable but indispensable to William. His liaison officer with them was his brother Louis, who signed with Brederode the famous Charter of the Beggars pledging the entire movement to inflict the maximum damage on Alba.

16. K vi, Jan 1571.

17. K vi 351.

18. Ibid., p. 390.

19. Wernham, *Before the Armada*, p. 318.

20. Ibid., pp. 320–2.

21. See Lovett, 'Don Luis de Requesens'.

22. K VI 484–97.

23. K VI 454, 484.

24. J. Ferguson, *The Scots Brigade in Holland* (1899) I 3–7.

25. K VI 730 f.

26. K VI 717, Apr 1573.

27. K VI, May–June 1573.

28. K VI 764, Herle to Burghley, June 1573.

29. Conyers Read, *Mr Secretary Walsingham and the Policy of Queen Elizabeth* (1925) I 312.

30. K VII 565.

31. See *Poets, Patrons and Professors*, by J. A. van Dorsten (Oxford and London, 1962).

32. Ibid., p. 8.

33. *Life of Sir Philip Sidney*, by Sir Fulke Greville, later Lord Brooke (1652), ed. Nowell Smith (1907) pp. 20–1.

34. D. Rogers to W. G. Buchanan, London, 30 Aug 1576 (*Buchanani Epistolae*, pp. 25–6.) Quoted by van Dorsten in *Poets, Patrons and Professors*, p. 46.

35. Ed. R. H. Tawney (1925).

36. K VII 383.

37. K VII 397, 27 Dec 1574.

38. K VII, 16 Apr 1575.

39. K VII 508–28.

40. K VII 592.

41. K VIII 38, R. Corbet, 16 Nov 1575.

42. See Lovett, 'Don Luis de Requesens'.

43. K VIII mmmxxii 68, John Hastings to Burghley 2 Dec 1575; B.M. Harley, 285, no. 15.

44. K VII 597. See also VIII 77 f. for the list of governors, commanders and counsellors for Philip in the Netherlands. With the exception of one German, Mansfeld, all were Spanish or Walloon nobles.

45. Groen van Prinsterer, *Archives*, v, 29 Nov 1575 (N.S.).

46. K VIII 48; Conyers Read, *Mr Secretary Walsingham*, I 314 f.

47. K VIII 113–18, 171.

48. Conyers Read, *Mr Secretary Walsingham*, I 322; *Cal. Spain*, 68–74, *State Papers (Elizabeth)* cxxxvi, f. 461.

49. See the article by Gaston Renson in *Miscellanea Historica in honorem Leonis van der Essen*, II (Brussels and Paris, 1947). Also the *Mémoires*, ed. A. L. P. de Robaulx de Soumoy (Brussels, 1872).

50. K VIII 250 ff. and 298.

51. K VIII 162–203.

52. See Ch. 4, p. 148, n. 66 below.

53. K VIII. See the *Journal* of Daniel Rogers, pp. 235, 239.

54. K VIII 250 ff.

55. K VIII 277–8.

56. K VIII 263–4.

F

57. K VIII 413. Chester was one of the early English volunteer officers in Zeeland in 1573: Markham, *The Fighting Veres*, p. 48.

58. K VIII 303, Walsingham to Davison, 12 Apr 1576.

Chapter 3

1. Pedro Aguilon had written to Philip's Secretary of State, Gabriel de Zayas, from Brussels on 20 Mar. He had been discussing with the other Flemish *commis des finances* in Flanders their complaints about the lax government of Alba and Requesens, especially their failure to enforce any audit of accounts and to give the nobles anything more than a minor role in affairs. He had asked the loyal Berlaymont who was fit to serve. Berlaymont had replied that the Duke of Aerschot was a good minister. 'I told him', wrote Aguilon, 'that he well knew that the duke was no man of affairs but only interested in his own indulgence and relaxation.' Berlaymont had then said that there was a growing feeling that the war could not be ended by conquest and force: even if His Majesty had to make some concessions 'afterwards in time everything can be reduced to a desirable state of affairs'. (Archivo de Simancas, Estado K, legajo 1537, f. 158, Aguilon – de Zayas.)

2. See Gachard, *Correspondance de Guillaume le Taciturne*, III 129, 147, 148.

3. K VIII 456.

4. Groen van Prinsterer, *Archives*, VI 116, St Aldegonde to John of Nassau, July 1576.

5. Ibid., pp. 117, 336, 448, 475, 513.

6. Groen van Prinsterer, *Archives*, V 470, Oct 1576.

7. Groen van Prinsterer, *Archives*, V 417–20, 541; VI 116–17, 215, 224–5, 227.

8. Groen van Prinsterer, *Archives*, V 505, 9 Nov 1576.

9. Groen van Prinsterer, *Archives*, VI 21, 141–4, Mar–Sept 1577.

10. Rogers to Walsingham, in K IX 416, July 1577.

11. For a good general account, dated but still valuable, see F. Rachfahl, *Wilhelm von Oranien und der Niederländische Aufstand* (Halle, 1908, and The Hague, 1924) I 241–76.

12. Leo von Rozmital, *Ritter- Hof- und Pilger-Reise* (Litterarischer Verin, Stuttgart, no. 7, 1843). Quoted by C. A. J. Armstrong in *Britain and the Netherlands*, ed. Bromley and Kossmann (1964) II, ch. 1 (see below).

13. See Armstrong, 'Had the Burgundian Government a Policy for the Nobility?', in *Britain and the Netherlands*, 9–29.

14. See F. W. N. Hugenholtz's two chapters in the *Algemene Geschiedenis der Nederlanden*, IV (Utrecht, 1952), and the same author's article in *Britain and the Netherlands*. Also H. Pirenne, *Histoire de Belgique* (Brussels, 1923) III 51–2.

15. Rachfahl, *Wilhelm von Oranien*, II 565–7.

16. H. G. Koenigsberger, 'Property and the Price Revolution (Hainault 1474–1573)', *Economic History Review* (Aug 1956).

17. *Papiers d'État du Cardinal Granvelle*, VII 18, 19 ff.

18. B.M. Additional MS. 28388, f. 1, Granvelle to Philip II, 22 June 1573. He probably converted Requesens to this view of the *political* character of the Revolt, in contrast to Alba, who held strongly that the origins were religious.

19. Rachfahl, *Wilhelm von Oranien*, I 210–11. Egmont's annual income was 33,000 ducats but he had incurred mortgages totalling almost one-third of this figure. His personal obligations at his death amounted to 125,000 ducats, or nearly four years' revenue. (Archivo General de Simancas Estado 4562, f. 77.)

20. Rennenberg's action has been the subject of much controversy. See Geyl, *The Revolt of the Netherlands*, pp. 176–7; also L. J. Rogier, 'Rennenberg's Afval', in *Annalen van het Thijmgenootschap*, XLV (1957) 125–34.

21. Sir George Clark, writing of William in his *Birth of the Dutch Republic*, has warned us that biography 'is always the most presumptuous of the arts' and that materials bearing directly on his character are rare. Yet Miss Wedgwood's biography (1944) seems to me in general to ring true. Equally, in a more analytical treatment, Professor C. J. Cadoux's *Philip of Spain and the Netherlands: An Essay on Moral Judgments in History* effectively exposes the absurd inconsistencies of William's recent critics like R. Trevor Davies, *The Golden Century of Spain* (1937) and W. T. Walsh, *Philip II* (1938). Nor does the attempt by E. Jones ('John Lingard and the Simancas Archives', in *Historical Journal* (1967) p. 66) at apologetics for Philip and the Inquisition seem to me any more successful.

22. K IX mmmdlxxix, Davison to Walsingham, 1577.

23. K VIII 319 ff. The memorandum is anonymous but it may have been prepared for Burghley by Davison or Wilson while in the Low Countries. Certainly it was the work of someone familiar with the arguments of the Prince.

24. K IX mmmccxlv, Wilson to Privy Council, 19 Nov 1576.

25. K IX mmmcclx, Wilson to Leicester, 3 Dec 1576.

26. K IX mmmcccxiv, Wilson to Burghley, 11 Jan 1577.

27. B.M. Galba C.V. f. 365, Wilson to Leicester, 30 Dec 1576.

28. K IX mmmccclxxix, Wilson to Walsingham, 1 Mar 1577.

29. K IX mmmcccxxix, Wilson to Walsingham, 24 Jan 1577.

30. K IX mmmcccc, the Queen to Wilson, 1 Apr 1577.

31. K IX mmmccccv, mmmccccxlii, mmmccccxliii.

32. H.M.C., *Marquis of Salisbury MSS*, pt II 151–4, Wilson to Leicester, 18 May 1577.

33. K IX mmmccccxvii, Wilson to Walsingham, 8 May 1577.

34. K IX mmmcccxciii, Rogers to Leicester, 20 July 1577.

35. K IX mmmdii, 'Instructions given by Her Majestie to Sir W. Davison . . . etc.', 27 July 1577.

36. K IX mmmdlxv, Davison to Leicester, 19 Sept 1577; K IX mmmdlxvii, Davison to Walsingham, 19 Sept 1577. This is one of Orange's most full and convincing arguments that he could defeat his rivals and overcome Don John provided he had the Queen's support.

37. See *Leicester's Triumph*, by R. C. Strong and J. A. van Dorsten (Oxford and Leyden, 1964) introduction. Also the declaration by William Fleetwood, a member of the Leicester connection, to Burghley: 'Every honest man here is desirous that Her Majestie should aide the Prince of Orange.' (Groen van Prinsterer, *Archives*, VI 409.)

38. K IX mmmdlix, memoir from Burghley to the Queen, 15 Sept 1577.

39. See Renson, in *Miscellanea Historica*.

40. K x mmmdclx, Davison to Leicester, 18 Nov 1577.

41. K x mmmdcvii, Leicester to Davison, 14 Oct 1577.

42. K x mmmdcxxviii, Davison to Burghley, 27 Oct 1577.

43. J. L. Motley, *The United Netherlands* (1904) I 99.

44. Groen van Prinsterer, *Archives*, VI, 9 Jan 1578.

45. K x mmmdcclxxiii, Davison to Walsingham, 3 Feb 1578.

46. K x mmmdcclxxx, Davison to Leighton, 12 Feb 1578.

47. Walsingham to Wilson, 20 Feb 1578, in Thomas Wright, *Queen Elizabeth and Her Times: A Series of Original Letters* (1838) II 69–77.

48. K x mmmdcccxi, Leicester to Davison, 9 Mar 1578.

49. Of all those whom she blamed for Mary, Queen of Scots' execution, Davison suffered worst. Sir John Neale has made a gallant attempt to exculpate Elizabeth for her extraordinary behaviour after the execution in his *Elizabeth and Her Parliaments*, pt II, ch. II: but not all his ingenious and learned advocacy seems to me to wash over the fact that she undoubtedly signed the Proclamation sentencing Mary and signed the death warrant. I can detect nothing thereafter which does her credit nor can I see any reason to argue that her hand was forced.

50. K x mmmdccxlv, Davison to Burghley, 29 Mar 1578. See also K x 374 and 380. Davison's arguments (shared by a number of English observers) are particularly interesting since much influential opinion amongst recent historians has tended to blame Prince Maurice for not being bolder in advancing against the enemy in Flanders in 1600 (e.g. Geyl, *The Revolt of the Netherlands*, p. 244). But precisely the same difficulties faced Maurice as had faced Don John and the Spanish commanders. See p. 60 below.

51. Groen van Prinsterer, *Archives*, VI 377.

52. J. L. Motley, *The Rise of the Dutch Republic* (Chandos Classics ed.) III 327–8.

53. K x mmmdcccxxxi, Rogers to Walsingham, 24 Mar 1578.

54. As William had foreseen, the royalists could now turn their sarcasm on him. As one balladist sang:
> Of the English Jezebel you get no audience,
> She leaves you in need without any defence,
> She has turned her coat. . . .

From *Politieke Balladen* in the *Vlaamsche Bibliophielen*, II vii 293, quoted in Geyl, *The Revolt of the Netherlands*, p. 182.

Chapter 4

1. *CSP (Foreign)*, 1577–9, ed. A. J. Butler (1901) no. 721.

2. Groen van Prinsterer, *Archives*, VI 470–1.

3. L. Stone, *Sir Horatio Palavicino* (1956) p. 70.
4. Motley, *The Rise of the Dutch Republic*, III 330.
5. K x mmmcmxviii, Davison to Walsingham, 17 May 1578.
6. K x mmmcccIxxxix, Walsingham to Davison, 2 May 1578.
7. K x mmmcmlxxiv, early July 1578.
8. See P. Henraad, *Histoire de l'artillerie en Belgique* (Brussels, 1867) pp. 114–15.
9. K x mmmcmlxxiv–mmmcmlxxvi. See also mmmmcxliv of 4 Sept (N.S.) where Thomas Digges, an expert in military engineering (see p. 95 n.), confirmed the great strength of Ghent to Burghley. Whatever was the cause of the fall of Ghent it was not the weakness of its fortifications.
10. K x mmmcmxciii, Walsingham to Leicester, 13 July 1578 (N.S.).
11. *CSP (Foreign)*, 1578–9, no. 139, Cobham to Burghley, 2 Aug 1578.
12. K x mmmmlx, Walsingham to Burleigh, 4 Aug 1578 (N.S.). For a good account of the battle, see L. van der Essen, *Alexandre Farnèse, prince de Parme*, I (Brussels, 1933).
13. K x mmmmcxliv, Digges to Burghley, 4 Sept 1578 (N.S.).
14. Ibid.
15. K x mmmmxxxiv, Walsingham to Leicester, 29 July 1578.
16. K x mmmmxcvii, Wilson to Walsingham, 18 Aug 1579.
17. K x mmmmcxxviii, Wilson to Cobham and Walsingham, 29 Aug 1578.
18. *Queen Elizabeth*, by Mandell Creighton (1899) p. 181.
19. K x mmmmclix, Walsingham to Wilson, 9 Sept 1578 (N.S.).
20. Walsingham to Hatton, 9 Sept 1578 (N.S.), in Wright, *Queen Elizabeth and Her Times*, II 93.
21. K x 763, Richard Topcliff to Earl of Shrewsbury, 30 Aug 1578. Topcliff was a leading member of the Puritan group of members in the House of Commons. For an account of his priest-hunting, see Neale, *Elizabeth and Her Parliaments*, p. 153 and *passim*.
22. Conyers Read, *Mr Secretary Walsingham*, I 416–22.
23. *CSP (Holland and Flanders, 1578–9)* IX 30, Walsingham to Sir Thomas Heneage, 2 Sept 1578.
24. See P. Bor, *Nederlantsche Oorloghen* (1621–30) XII 1004, 1005.
25. According to Strada, x 516, 519 (*Relación de la enfermedad y muerte*), the reason was that it cost Philip less to do it in this way rather than face a public and highly ceremonial journey.
26. Van der Essen, *Alexandre Farnèse*, I 5, VII, VIII.
27. *CSP (Foreign)*, 1578–9, 345, Wilson to Davison, 4 Nov 1578.
28. K xi mmmmcccxcv, Davison to Walsingham, 13 Feb 1579.
29. K xi mmmmcccxv, Wilson to Davison, 8 Dec 1578.
30. Groen van Prinsterer, *Archives*, IV; quoted in Motley, *The United Netherlands*, I 22. For the full story of Farnese's negotiations with the Walloon nobles, see the *Reconciliation des Provinces Wallones*, I–V (Archives du Royaume, Brussels); the *Liber Relationum*, MS. II 1155 (Bibliothèque Royale de Bruxelles); *Bulletins de la Commission Royale d'Histoire*, LXXXII (1913) 389 f.; correspondence of Farnese with Count

of Hennin (1578–85); la Comtesse Marie de Villermont, *Le Duc Charles de Croy et d'Arschot* (1923); la Princesse P. de C. Chimay, *Recueil de lettres à et par Charles de Croy* (1913); also the *Bulletins* LXXXVI (1922) and LXXXI (1912), for articles by E. Dony on the Chimay-Croy archives.

31. Discussions had been in progress between the Walloon States since October 1578. See Groen van Prinsterer, *Archives*, VI 469.

32. Pirenne (preface to van der Essen, *Alexandre Farnèse*) remarks that Arras reunited the south in a 'Belgique monarchique et catholique'. This is surely premature? The great battles of Maastricht and Antwerp had yet to be fought.

33. *CSP* (*Foreign*), 1578–9 (1903) 523, Fremyn to Davison, 17 Jan 1579.

34. Van der Essen, *Alexandre Farnèse*, II, ch. VI *passim*. For the effects on Orange's prestige at Ghent after Elizabeth's desertion, and the decomposition of the rebel party there, see the still very valuable account in B. de Jonghe's *Gendsche Geschiedenissen* (1781) II 260–76.

35. Davison to Walsingham, probably early July 1579, Wright, *Queen Elizabeth and Her Times*, II 644–9.

36. Archivio di Stato, Parma, Carteggio Farnesiano, Busta 128 (Spagna 5) (unfoliated), Parma to Don Bernadino de Mendoza, 3 Oct 1580.

37. Printed in Bor, *Nederlantsche Oorloghen*, XVI 276–80. For a full summary, see Motley, *The Rise of the Dutch Republic*, III 495–8.

38. Van der Essen, *Alexandre Farnèse*, III.

39. See L. P. Gachard, *Correspondance de Philippe II sur les affaires des Pays-Bas* (Brussels, 1848–79); tome II, 1580–4, ed. J. Lefèvre (Brussels, 1953) pp. 250–69.

40. See Griffiths, 'The Revolutionary Character of the Revolt of the Netherlands', in *Comparative Studies in Society and History*, II. The writer examines the claims of the Revolt to be 'revolutionary', discerning three phases of classic development, from aristocratic via extreme democratic to the consolidation of forces in a 'Third Estate' phase. Like Wittman (see below, p. 153, n. 4) this account, though carefully constructed, pays little attention to any but purely internal events.

41. The explanation (Geyl, *The Revolt of the Netherlands*, pp. 176–7) that Rennenberg's 'treason' at Groningen was also an 'act of policy' provides no convincing defence of what still remained also an act of treachery. Treachery is hardly diminished by the fact that it is committed by more than one offender.

42. Motley, *The Rise of the Dutch Republic*, III 366–7.

43. For the phase of popular Calvinist domination in Ghent, see J. E. Nève de Mévergnies, *Gand en république. La domination calviniste à Gand 1577–1584* (Ghent, 1940). Also Tibor Wittmann, *Les Gueux dans les 'Bonnes Villes' de Flandre 1577–1584*.

44. Motley, *The Rise of the Dutch Republic*, III 612; Bibliothèque Royale de Bruxelles, 11 July 1584, report by the Greffier Aertssens.

45. *Apologie du Prince d'Orange* (Leyden, 1581) pp. 107–9.

46. See Gachard–Lefèvre, *Correspondance de Philippe II*, tome IV,

no. 1046, for a report of Apr 1596 by Estebán de Ibarra on the Netherlands nobility.

47. Creighton, *Queen Elizabeth*, p. 181. See also Wernham, *Before the Armada*, p. 220, and his chapter in *Britain and the Netherlands*, ed. Bromley and Kossmann.

48. *State Papers*, Herle to the Queen, 22 July/1 Aug 1584.

49. See, e.g., van der Essen, *Alexandre Farnèse*, and Motley, *The United Netherlands*, I.

50. Creighton, *Queen Elizabeth*, p. 218.

51. Mattingley, *The Defeat of the Armada*, p. 40.

52. Wagenaar, *Vaderlandsche Historiën* (1790–6) VIII 50.

53. *CSP (Foreign)*, 1584–5, pp. 241–2, Walsingham to Davison, 14 Jan 1585.

54. *Memorie van Ortel en de Grijze*, 24 Mar 1585, Algemeen Rijksarchief, The Hague, Lias Engeland, no. 5880.

55. Ortel to States-General, 8 May 1585, Algemeen Rijksarchief, The Hague, Loketkas Engeland 12576, 2.

56. See Winston S. Churchill, *The Second World War* (1949) II, ch. xx, for the details of the arrangements by which Britain had to lease West Indies bases in return for obsolete destroyers. H.M.C., *Lord de Lisle and Dudley MSS.*, II and III, contain much valuable material on relations between Elizabeth and the Netherlands from the start of the revolt onwards. Dr W. A. Shaw's introduction to vol. IIII (1936) is a ripely patriotic essay from which Elizabeth emerges as a character of transparent virtue, the Dutch as unprincipled and untrustworthy schemers. The delay in completing a treaty is laid entirely at the door of the Dutch though no evidence is produced for their alleged delays in June. The basic fact that the relief of Antwerp was as vital to the defence of England as of the Netherlands is ignored and the Queen's benevolence is regarded as purest altruism. Yet Dr Shaw's interpretation differs in one important respect from that of other admirers of the Queen. He does not either blame or praise her for her parsimony. On the contrary, he sees her as 'prodigal of her treasure, careful not of her money but only of the blood of Englishmen': introduction, p. lxxvii.

57. *CSP (Foreign)*, 1584–5, Gilpin to Walsingham, 24 Apr.

58. *CSP (Foreign)*, 1584–5, p. 427, Ortel to Walsingham, 25 Apr 1585.

59. Van der Essen, *Alexandre Farnèse*, IV 146 f.

60. *Discours de la Royne*, 5–13 Aug 1585. Algemeen Rijksarchief, The Hague, Loketkas Engeland 12548, 54.

61. Van der Essen, *Alexandre Farnèse*, IV 146 f. Negotiations between the defenders of Antwerp and Parma had been going on for a month. The news that the defence had collapsed reached London five days before the Treaty of Nonsuch was signed and two days after the official surrender to Parma: *CSP (Foreign)*, 1584–5, 688–90.

62. Motley, *The United Netherlands*, I 333, 334.

63. Geyl, *The Revolt of the Netherlands* (1966 ed.) pp. 198–9. Dr Rowse defends the Queen against what he calls Geyl's injustices in *The Expansion of Elizabethan England*, ch. x.

64. *CSP (Foreign)*, 1584–5, p. 660.

65. *CSP (Foreign)*, 1584–5, pp. 669–81, Norris to Privy Council, 21 Aug 1585. Norris landed with his troops on Walcheren on 19 Aug. In fairness to the Queen it must be said that the constitutional checks under which the Dutch negotiators were compelled to act would have strained the patience of a far more equable prince. She never seemed to understand – or any rate never admitted – that they were strictly bound by the local authorities whom they represented not to vary or exceed their instructions.

66. He was a relation by marriage of the Earl of Northumberland, probably implicated in the Northern rising. Immediately afterwards he was sent to London and engaged by Burghley to spy on the Catholic prisoners in the Marshalsea prison. Froude described him as 'poor, cunning, unprincipled and dissolute'. (*History of England* (1870) x 213 f.) There is no reason to suspect him of exaggerating.

67. B.M. Cotton MSS., Galba C. vi, ff. 119–20, 122–3; *S.P.(P.R.O.)*, 1584–5, xII 181, 32. Also Conyers Read, *Lord Burghley and Queen Elizabeth* (1960) pp. 319 ff. From start to finish, it took exactly a year to get the Dutch request for help incorporated in the Treaty of Nonsuch. See *CSP (Foreign)*, 1584–5, pp. 699–710. Burghley defended himself against the charges conveyed by Herle with some vigour, blaming the hesitations and delays on the Queen herself and confessing he was powerless to deal with her. See Froude, *History of England*, xII 130–3 and n. 131–2.

68. See her note to the States-General in *CSP (Foreign)*, 1584–5, p. 678, and the letter from the Earl of Shrewsbury's son to his father, 26 Aug: 'Her Majestie was greatly troubled with the rendering up of Antwerp.' (*Talbot Papers*, Longleat, 1, f. 107; Motley, *The United Netherlands*, 1 372.)

Chapter 5

1. J. Du Mont, *Corps Universal Diplomatique*, v 454.
2. Bor, *Nederlantsche Oorloghen*, 11 667–71.
3. *CSP (Foreign)*, 1585–6, Walsingham to Davison, 5/15 Sept 1585.
4. B.M. Galba D. ii, f. 141 M.S., Willoughby to Leicester, Sept 1587. See also Conyers Read, *Lord Burghley and Queen Elizabeth*, pp. 396, 460.
5. *Life of Sidney*, by Fulke Greville, p. 16.
6. See J. U. Nef, *Cultural Foundations of Industrial Civilisation* (1958) p. 12, for a striking example of Buckhurst's grasp of trade statistics and how to use them as a basis of government policy.
7. See *Knole and the Sackvilles* (1922) by Victoria Sackville-West.
8. Stow, *Chronicle*, 711.
9. *CSP*, 1585–6, Wilsford to Walsingham, 18 Dec 1585.
10. *CSP*, 1585–6, Cavendish to Burghley, 18 Mar 1586.
11. *Correspondence of Robert Dudley, Earl of Leicester during his Government of the Low Countries in the years 1585 and 1586*, ed. John Bruce (1844) pp. 30–2.
12. Motley, *The United Netherlands*, i, ch. vii; Strong and van Dorsten, *Leicester's Triumph*, p. 60.

13. Wilsford to Walsingham, 15/25 Dec 1585. Wilford to Burghley, 18/28 Dec 1585.

14. Bruce, *Leicesters Correspondence*: 'Instructions' and 'Advice of the Commissioners to Leicester', Dec 1585.

15. *CSP (Foreign)*, 1585–6, Leicester to Burghley and Walsingham, 15 Mar 1586.

16. Bruce, *Leicester's Correspondence*, p. 58, 14/24 Jan 1586.

17. *CSP*, 1585–6, Leicester to Davison, 11/21 Jan 1586.

18. *Resolutions of the States General*, 4 Feb 1586; Bor, *Nederlantsche Oorloghen*, III 688, 689.

19. Bruce, *Leicester's Correspondence*, pp. 113–14, 11/14 Feb 1586.

20. *CSP*, 1585-6, 13/23 Feb 1586.

21. Parma to Philip II, 30 Mar 1586, in Gachard-Lefèvre, *Correspondance de Philippe II*, tome III, no. 217.

22. Ibid.

23. *CSP*, North to Burghley, 29 May 1586.

24. Bruce, *Leicester's Correspondence*, 8/18 May 1586.

25. Ibid., 30 Apr–10 May 1586.

26. *CSP*, 1585–6, Sidney to Burghley, 18 Mar 1586.

27. *CSP*, 1586–7, T. Cecil to Burghley, 21/31 July 1586.

28. The *Journal* of Stephen Burrough, Admiral of Leicester's fleet, shows that the quarrels had begun even before the force set out from Harwich. See introduction to *Leicester's Correspondence*.

29. W. Gray, *Life of Sidney* (1829) p. 290.

30. *CSP*, *Advertisement of the Present State of These Low Countries*, by T. Digges, 3/13 Mar 1586; also Digges to Walsingham, 2/12 Jan 1586.

31. *CSP*, 158–56, North to Burghley, 29 May–8 June.

32. Bor, *Nederlantsche Oorloghen*, XXIII 98.

33. For a full account of the struggle for power and the theoretical basis of the claims put forward by the parties, see Everhard van Reyd, *Voornaamste Geschiedenissen (1566–1601)* (1650) v *passim*; Grimston, *History of the Netherlands*, XIII 788 ff.; Bor, *Nederlantsche Oorloghen* III; P. C. Hooft, *Nederlandsche Histooriën* and *Vervolgh der Nederlandsche Histooriën* (1642–54) XXI–XXVII; *CSP (Foreign)*, 1585–6, 1586–7, 1587–8 *passim*; Bruce, *Leicester's Correspondence*, *passim*.

34. *CSP (Foreign)*, 1586–7, Clerk to Burghley, 11 Aug 1586.

35. Bruce, *Leicester's Correspondence*, no. 263; quoted in Strong and van Dorsten, *Leicester's Triumph*, p. 79.

36. Van Reyd, *Voornaamste Geschiedenissen (1566–1601)* v 85: van Reyd was Secretary to William Louis of Nassau (q.v., p. 110); *CSP (Foreign)*, 1586–7, J. Norris to Burghley, 21 Jan 1587.

37. *CSP (Foreign)*, 1586–7, Conway to Walsingham, 28 Jan 1587.

38. B.M. Galba C. XI, f. 327, Walsingham to Leicester, 17 Apr 1587.

39. Cf. the estimates of Calvinist numbers by the Roman Catholic historian L. F. Rogier, *Geschiedenis van het Katholicisme in Noord-Nederland in de 16e en 17e Eeuw*, 2 vols (Amsterdam, 1945) *passim*.

40. Buckhurst to the Queen, Apr–May 1587; *Cabala or Mysteries of States*, pp. 11–37.

41. *CSP*, 1587, Walsingham to Wilkes, 2 May 1587.

42. *CSP*, 1587, Wilkes to Walsingham, 8 June 1587.

43. Motley, *The United Netherlands*, II 311.

44. *CSP*, 1587, Leicester to Atye, 4 Dec 1587; Stow, *Chronicle*, 713.

45. See Motley, *The United Netherlands*, II *passim*; Sir J. E. Neale, 'Elizabeth and the Netherlands 1586–7' in *Essays in Elizabethan History* (1958), a careful review of vol. XXI (II and III) of the *Calendar of State Papers*; Dietz, *English Public Finance 1485–1641*, II, esp. chs III and XX; Wernham, in *Elizabethan Government and Society*, ed. Bindoff *et al.*

46. 'I can see no trace of financial or organising ability in his action, as there is no trace of statesmanship. And duty sat lightly upon him. Rank he possessed but no other quality for his office. Even honesty . . . was absent. His reputation is deservedly low.' (Neale, in *Essays in Elizabethan History*).

47. Even the account of Leicester's military operations and qualifications by Markham, an unusually sympathetic critic, does little more than call attention to his stupidity and incompetence: *The Fighting Veres*, pp. 72, 73, 97 (n.), 113, 114.

48. Bruce, *Leicester's Correspondence*, 237–9. Apropos of her treatment of the French, see Walsingham's letters to Leicester, 8–10 Apr 1587 (B.M. Galba C. XI, ff. 319–21).

49. *CSP (Foreign)*, 1587, 125.

50. *The Revolt of the Netherlands*, p. 215.

51. The crucial role played by chronic mutiny in the Spanish Army's campaigns is fully analysed in Dr Geoffrey Parker's thesis 'The Spanish Road'.

52. See Mattingley, *The Defeat of the Spanish Armada*. Motley's account in *The United Netherlands* is still useful, especially on Parma's problems.

53. *The Defeat of the Spanish Armada*, p. 82.

54. *The Revolt of the Netherlands*, p. 202.

55. The original estimates were 150 great ships, 40 galleys, 300 supply ships, 30,000 sailors and 64,000 soldiers. The revised figures were 68 fighting ships, 64 supply ships, 19,000 soldiers. 44 ships reached home, the rest were lost in action or by shipwreck. (Mattingley, *The Defeat of the Spanish Armada*, p. 80.)

56. Gachard–Lefèvre, *Correspondance de Philippe II*, tome III, nos 599, 600.

57. Conyers Read, *Lord Burghley and Queen Elizabeth*, p. 424.

58. Mattingley, *The Defeat of the Spanish Armada*, p. 296.

59. Motley, *United Netherlands*, II 500, quoting letter from Williams to Walsingham, July 1588. See Conyers Read, *Lord Burghley and Queen Elizabeth*, esp. pp. 424–31, for Burghley's strategic intelligence and his orders to Leicester and Walsingham.

Chapter 6

1. B.M. Cotton MSS., Galba C. v, f. 65. See also Conyers Read, *Lord Burghley and Queen Elizabeth*, pp. 463 ff. See also Sir Walter Raleigh's

comments in the 1593 Parliament: S. D'Ewes, *Journal of all the Parliaments* (1682) 509.

2. For Willoughby's achievement, see Conyers Read, *Lord Burghley and Queen Elizabeth*, p. 396.

3. *CSP (Foreign)* (Jan–July 1589), 272, p. 195.

4. *Report on the MSS of the Earl of Ancaster* (H.M.C., 1907), George Gilpin to Lord Willoughby, 8 Apr 1589.

5. *CSP (Foreign)* (Aug 1589–June 1590) I *passim*.

6. L. van der Essen, 'Le Testament politique d'Alexandre Farnèse', *Bulletin de la Commission Royale d'Histoire*, 86 (1922) 171–215; also 'Schets van Champagny's jeugd 1536–74' and 'Champagny in 1576' in *Handelingen der Zuid Nederlandse Maatschappij*, VI (1952) and XIII (1959).

7. *Discours du Seigneur de Champagny sur les affaires des Pays-Bas*, Dec 1589, Bibliothèque de Bourgogne, MS. 12,962.

8. See the full and excellent discussion in Jan den Tex, *Oldenbarneveldt* (Haarlem, 1962) II *passim*; also *CSP (Foreign)* (Jan–July 1589) Introduction.

9. In his review of Meester den Tex's biography of Oldenbarneveldt in the *English Historical Review* (Apr 1965), Sir George Clark writes that Oldenbarneveldt abandoned 'the illusory project of uniting the Netherlands from Groningen to Cambrai'. If he did, it was only after 1600 and then with the utmost reluctance.

10. See Snapper, *Oorlogsnvloeden op de Overzeese Handel van Holland 1551–1719*, pp. 39–42; also L. Mulder's introduction to the *Journaal van Anthonis Duyck (1591–1602)* (The Hague, 1862).

11. They were related by marriage to the famous Springs of Lavenham. See Markham, *The Fighting Veres*, pp. 1–27.

12. *The Commentaries of Sr Francis Vere* (Cambridge, 1647).

13. See, e.g., Markham, *The Fighting Veres*; Rowse, *The Expansion of Elizabethan England*, ch. x *passim*.

14. For a full account, see Markham, *The Fighting Veres*. I agree with Dr Rowse that Motley was less than fair to Vere, but he never impugned his courage or efficiency. Symbolically, Francis Vere's tomb in Westminster Abbey is modelled after the great marble tomb of Engelbert of Nassau at Breda.

15. Thomas Fuller, *The History of the Worthies of England* (1811 ed.) II 227–9.

16. Roger Williams, *The Actions of the Low Countries* (1618).

17. See Lindsay Boynton, *The Elizabethan Militia 1558–1638* (1967) p. 90. Mr Boynton stresses the vital need in the English army for a professional attitude to military organisation based on Continental standards. The new criteria of specialised expertise and the improved training of English officers were largely based on the experience of the Low Countries down to the Civil War. See e.g. the biographies of the leading officers in the Civil War in P. Young, *Edgehill 1642* (1967) part 3; also Markham, *The Fighting Veres*, pp. 456 ff. Not everyone agreed. Sir John Smythe, a conservative and a Roman Catholic, in his *Proême Dedicatorie to the*

Nobilitie of the Realme of England (1589–90), attacks the English expeditionary force, as a 'tumultuarie and disordered' body, productive only of indiscipline, corruption, drunkenness and brutality. A perfunctory exculpation of Leicester from his general charges did not free him from royal displeasure. He ended his days lamenting his lack of employment (he had earlier fought for the Duke of Alba) and a last unhappy indiscretion – a ridiculous miniature rebellion in Essex – landed him in gaol. Ironically he obtained his freedom only by pleading drunkenness as his defence.

18. *Report on the MSS of the Earl of Ancaster*, Lord Willoughby to Lord Burghley, 28 May 1589.

19. *CSP (Foreign)* (Aug 1589–June 1590), H. 64, H. 479, H. 534.

20. See above, p. 107 and *Ancaster MSS, passim.*

21. *CSP (Foreign)*, 1589–90, A. 7, 24 June. See also Den Tex, *Oldenbarneveldt*, II, ch. XXIII, pp. 100–18; R. B. Wernham, 'The Mission of Thomas Wilkes to the United Provinces in 1590' in *Studies presented to Sir Hilary Jenkinson* (1957).

22. Den Tex, *Oldenbarneveldt*, pp. 118 f.

23. For the Queen's own view of herself as a kind of supreme commander, see Wernham in *Britain and the Netherlands*, ed. Bromley and Kossmann, pp. 36–7.

24. A letter from Bodley to Burghley (17 May 1591) describes the ingenious stratagem by which Zutfen Sconce was surprised by an advance party disguised as peasants selling provisions. Bodley attributes the successful ruse to Francis Vere. So, needless to say, did Vere. 'I chose a good number of lusty and hardy young Souldiers, the most of which I apparelled like the country-women of those parts . . .'. Armed with pistols, short swords and daggers under their skirts, they rushed the gate when it was opened. 'By which means the siege of the Town afterwards proved the shorter.' (Vere, *Commentaries*, pp. 17–18.) The Netherlands chroniclers suggest that the scheme was contrived by Maurice and the capture of the fort was the work of the States' forces. For Bodley's letter see Wright, *Queen Elizabeth and Her Times*, II 412–13.

25. Markham, *The Fighting Veres*, pp. 171–5, 178, 272–7. Full details are to be found in Grimston, *History of the Netherlands, passim.*

26. Aksel E. Christensen, *The Dutch Trade to the Baltic about 1600* (Copenhagen and The Hague, 1941), esp. pp. 17–33 and chs V, VII and IX.

27. See J. A. Faber, 'The Decline of the Baltic Grain Trade in the Second Half of the Seventeenth Century' in *Acta Historiae Nederlandica* (Leiden, 1966) pp. 108–32; also Charles Wilson, *The Dutch Republic and the Civilization of the Seventeenth Century* (London and New York, 1968) pp. 22–41.

28. Fuentes to Philip, 28 Mar 1595, Gachardi–Lefèvre, *Correspondance de Philippe II*, pp. 280 f.

29. Ibid., tome IV, no. 1046.

30. *Discours du Seigneur de Champagny sur les affaires des Pays-Bas*, Bibliothèque Royale de Bruxelles 17.361–421, ff. 251–66

31. Geyl thought Maurice missed the last great chance of uniting the

two halves of the whole through excessive caution in 1600 (*The Revolt of the Netherlands*, p. 244). Does not this disregard the fact that this was still siege warfare? Davison's dictum (Ch. 3, p. 60) that one good town well defended could ruin a mighty army was as true as ever and Maurice was the last man to forget it.

32. See Motley, *The United Netherlands*, III 450–1, 464–5.

33. M. L. van Deventer, *Gedenkstukken van Johan van Oldenbarneveldt* (The Hague, 1860–5) II 108–19. See also *The Papers of George Wyatt Esquire*, ed. D. M. Loades (Camden Fourth Series, Royal Historical Society, 1968).

34. Caron to States-General, Nov 1597, Deventer, *Gedenkstukken*, II 161–4. See also the Queen's letter of 14 Aug 1596 to the Admiral commanding the Dutch fleet in the attack on Cadiz which radiated goodwill. Bor, *Nederlantsche Oorloghen*, IV 235: translated into Flemish; Motley, *The United Netherlands*, III 442.

35. See Den Tex, *Oldenbarneveldt*, ch. 9, for the full account of the negotiations.

36. Deventer, *Gedenkstukken*, II 290–3.

Conclusion

1. *Transactions of the Royal Historical Society*, Fifth Series, XVII (1967).

2. See Bruce's introduction to the *Leicester Correspondence*, which scouts the idea that the Queen was subject to secret influences, e.g. in refusing to accept Leicester's assumption of the absolute governorship. The decisions (Bruce believed) were the Queen's own.

3. For a Victorian eulogy, see J. R. Green, *Short History of the English People* (1874; 1929 ed.) pp. 370–6.

4. Tibor Wittman's *Les Gueux dans les 'Bonnes Villes' de Flandre 1577–1584* seeks and finds the causes of the 'crisis' in the south in the decay of the Old Draperies in the towns, especially Ghent. That economic factors played a role in the confusions of Flanders there is no doubt, but this study seems to exaggerate the influence of economic and internal factors at the expense of political, religious, social and external factors, including events in France and England which powerfully affected the course of the Revolt. There were differences between north and south, but the leaders in both areas were noble or merchant-patrician and Mr Wittman seems to me to exaggerate the 'revolutionary' character of the northern bourgeoisie. In the north as in the south, revolutionary ardour was more often Calvinist than bourgeois. Nor is adequate attention given to the effects on both areas of the large migrations of traders and workers. The failure in the south cannot be explained except in relation to the situation of the Netherlands as a whole in Europe, with all the contingencies that implied.

5. Rowse, *The Expansion of Elizabethan England*, p. 414.

6. See D. B. Horn, *Great Britain and Europe in the Eighteenth Century* (1967), esp. pp. 95–7; P. Geyl, *The Netherlands in the Seventeenth Century* (1964) pp. 38 f.; Charles Wilson, *Economic History and the Historian*

(1969), for the essay on 'Taxation and the Decline of Empires' first read as a paper to the Royal Historical Society at Utrecht, 1962.

7. See also A. J. Veendaal, *Het Engels-Nederlands Condominium in de Zuiderlijke Nederlanden* (Utrecht, 1945) *passim*.

8. See especially Wernham, *Before the Armada*; 'Elizabethan War Aims and Strategy' in *Elizabethan Government and Society*, ed. Bindoff *et al.*, pp. 340–68; 'English Policy and the Revolt of the Netherlands' in *Britain and the Netherlands*, ed. Bromley and Kossmann, pp. 29–40.

9. *Britain and the Netherlands*, pp. 30–2.

10. Dr Lovett in his thesis on Requesens emphasises that Philip never abandoned Alba's doctrine that the Netherlands must be suppressed by force. Even Requesens fairly quickly abandoned the slightly more liberal, if equivocal, ideas with which he began his period of office.

11. See 'English Policy and the Revolt of the Netherlands' in *Britain and the Netherlands*, ed. Bromley and Kossmann, p. 33. As Professor Wernham says, almost half a century was to pass after Henry IV's conversion to Roman Catholicism in 1593 before France regained enough unity and strength to threaten the Spanish Netherlands seriously.

12. *Lettre de la Sérénissime Reine d'Angleterre aux États-Généraux*, 6 Feb 1582, *Depêchen Boek der Staten-General*, Algemeen Rijksarchief, The Hague.

13. William's predicament and the duress under which he acted in the Anjou affair have been well set out by C. V. Wedgwood in her *William the Silent* (1944), esp. ch. IX.

14. See E. M. W. Tillyard, *Shakespeare's History Plays* (1944) pp. 59–70; also the same author's *Elizabethan World Picture* (1943); Beckingsale, *Elizabeth I*, pp. 102–3.

15. Gachard–Lefèvre, *Correspondance de Philippe II*, tome III, no. 217, 30 Mar 1586.

16. *Discours de Menin: Audience à Greenwich*, Algemeen Rijksarchief, The Hague, Loketkas 124548, 56.

17. Dietz, *English Public Finance 1485–1641*, II, chs III and XX *passim*.

18. *Elizabethan Government and Society*, p. 350.

19. *Hansard*, 12 Nov 1936.

20. See John Aubrey, *Brief Lives*, ed. A. Powell (1949) p. 317.

21. See B. W. Beckingsale, *Burghley, Tudor Statesman* (1967) p. 161; Motley, *The United Netherlands*, I 552, 555, 557, II 336.

22. Beckingsale, *Elizabeth I*, p. 121.

23. *English Historical Review* (Jan 1968) in a review of Professor Wernham's *Before the Armada*.

24. Smit, in *Britain and the Netherlands* (1960), ed. Bromley and Kossmann, p. 25.

25. See P. Geyl, *Orange and Stuart* (1969), esp. ch. II.

26. For a general discussion by Professor Schöffer, see 'Protestantism in Flux during the Revolt of the Netherlands' in *Britain and the Netherlands* (1964), ed. Bromley and Kossmann.

27. The idea, still current, that the Anglo-Dutch sea wars of 1652 and 1664 are proof of a Dutch 'threat' to English security is merely a

relic of insular history. Pieter Geyl's *Orange and Stuart*, chs I–III, reveals how personal and contingent were the factors leading to these wars. In *Profit and Power* (1957) I have dealt with the economic 'forces' leading to the wars. They came largely from an interested and misguided English minority, wisely repudiated by Cromwell and resisted for several years by Charles II. There was nothing predestined about them: they were in fact an aberration and a costly one, properly regretted later.

28. Dr Rowse believes that Ireland provides the only instance where the Queen's parsimony in the middle decades of her reign created the need for larger outlays later. Certainly her policy of 'indirect rule' with its accompaniment of atrocities, depopulation and starvation was a disaster. But the case of Ireland seems to me to run parallel to that of the Netherlands. And the Dutch after all were only *borrowing* money and supplies.

29. The Parliaments of 1589, 1593 and 1601 were equally generous. See Neale, *Elizabeth and Her Parliaments 1584–1601*, p. 413. Members like Throckmorton who spoke out too boldly for a more positive policy on the Low Countries were reproved or imprisoned: ibid., ch. IV.

30. See Elton, *England Under the Tudors*, ch. XIII.

31. *State Papers (Foreign)*, Digges to Walsingham, 2/12 Jan 1585.

32. See Markham, *The Fighting Veres*, ch. v, 'The English Volunteers'.

33. Wernham, in *Britain and the Netherlands*, ed. Bromley and Kossmann, p. 40; see also *Elizabethan Government and Society*, ed. Bindoff *et al.*, pp. 345–6.

34. As Professor Wernham says, Elizabeth had helped 'to put the French monarchy on its feet again' (*Elizabethan Government and Society*), but it is not clear that this was necessarily a service to international peace.

35. Williams, ibid.

36. Wernham, ibid., p. 368.

37. Creighton, *Queen Elizabeth* (1911 ed.) p. 218.

38. Or Walsingham's remarks on 'our half-doing': see above, Ch. 5, p. 105; Mattingley, *The Defeat of the Spanish Armada*, p. 296.

A Note on Sources

THE systematic exploration of the European archives bearing on the Netherlands Revolt began with a prodigious burst of energy in the second quarter of the nineteenth century and has continued steadily into the twentieth. So that when John Lothrop Motley completed the first part of his study of the Revolt in 1856 (*The Rise of the Dutch Republic*) he was already able to draw on the pioneer work of Dutch and Belgian scholars of whom Groen van Prinsterer, R. C. Bakhuizen van den Brink and L. P. Gachard were the most eminent. Groen's edition of the *Archives ou correspondance inédite de la Maison d'Orange-Nassau* (1552–84 in 9 volumes with Supplement, 1835–47) was already available. Gachard's *Correspondance de Guillaume le Taciturne* came out in 1851 (Brussels). The *Correspondance d'Alexandre Farnèse, prince de Parme, avec Philippe II 1578–1581* followed in 1853. Indeed, the prodigious labours of this master-builder among archivists were proceeding steadily on many fronts between 1847 and 1880. Between 1861 and 1866 the *Actes des États Généraux 1576/1585* were published. Between 1848 and 1879 Gachard produced five volumes of the *Correspondance de Philippe II sur les affaires des Pays-Bas*. (They were continued by J. Lefèvre in supplementary volumes published in 1940.)

But Motley did not have to await publication. He had advance access to Gachard's work, including that which he had carried out in the archives of Brussels as well as in the archives of Paris and Simancas. In the second half of the nineteenth century the largest additions to the printed sources bearing on the Netherlands Revolt were the eleven great volumes of *Relations politiques des Pays-Bas et de l'Angleterre* (1882–1900, Brussels). The editor was Baron J. B. M. C. Kervyn de Lettenhove. At the same time the *Calenders of State Papers (Foreign)* began to emerge steadily from 1863 onwards.

These older printed sources, dating from the historiographical revolution of the nineteenth century, have been supplemented in the twentieth century by the continuing work of Dutch and Belgian scholars. Amongst them are Dr N. Japikse's edition of the *Resolutiën van de Staten Generaal* (1918) and *Correspondentie van Willem I* (The Hague, 1934) and Dr H. Brugman's *Correspondentie van Robert Dudley, Graaf van Leycester* (3 vols, The Hague, 1931).

For commercial relations, and especially the growing evidence of difficulties between the Merchant Adventurers and Antwerp under Spanish rule, see Dr H. J. Smit's *Bronnen tot de geschiedenis van den handel met Engeland, Schotland en Ierland* (Rijksgeschiedkundige

Publicatiën, The Hague, 1928). Of the Historical Manuscripts Commission's publications, the three volumes of the manuscripts of Lord De Lisle and Dudley (ed. Dr W. A. Shaw, 1936) contain evidence on Anglo-Dutch diplomatic exchanges, especially in relation to the defence and fall of Antwerp. (The editorial opinions are narrowly and determinedly insular and should be read critically.)

Published collections of this magnitude and complexity require to be read and re-read in the changing light of the research done in recent years on every aspect of the second half of the sixteenth century – Dutch, Belgian, Spanish, French and English. No prolonged inquiry is necessary to discover that (as usual) considerable tracts of, e.g., Kervyn de Lettenhove's eleven volumes still remain virgin territory, though some of the inaccuracies of the original transcriptions have been corrected by more recent editors of the English State Papers.

To all these must be added the vast collections of printed pamphlets and chronicles. The Royal Library at The Hague contains not only the so-called Duncan Collection but a rich hoard of contemporary printed works relevant to the Revolt and England's role in it (see the Catalogue of 1889 by Dr W. P. C. Knuttel). The chronicles of Strada Bor, P. C. Hooft, van Meteren, Wagenaar and van Reyd, though much used, are still a necessary source, as is Edward Grimeston's *A General Historie of the Netherlands* (1627) and the *Commentaries* of Sir Francis Vere (1657 ed.).

The European archives are rich in documentary collections bearing on the Revolt and its international repercussions. The sources concerning the relations of the States-General and the English government are preserved at the Algemeen Rijksarchief, and I am particularly grateful to Mev. M. A. P. Meilink-Roelofsz, Keeper of the First Section, for her generous assistance in helping me to locate evidence relating to the events of the 1580s. The manuscripts section of the Bibliothèque Royale in Brussels is particularly valuable for information about Champagny and is richly supplemented by documents in the Collection Granvelle in the archives at Besançon (see the *Catalogue général des manuscrits des bibliothèques publiques de France*: Besançon II, part I (Paris, 1900), especially vols XLII and LXIII–LXVIII). Other private archives relating to the Lalaing, Lannoy and Croy families and to the Order of the Golden Fleece are still in the private possession of the owners or trustees or have been transferred to the archives at Mons.

The largest source of information about Philippe II's relations with his Netherlands governors and officials is of course the archives at Simancas. These are supplemented by the Farnese Collection in the Archivio di Stato at Parma – alas! in lamentable condition. (The remaining collection at Naples was destroyed in 1943.) The British Museum also has useful material relating to the Revolt, especially among the Additional and Cotton Manuscripts. (Detailed references will be found in the notes to my text.)

The debate among Netherlands historians about the Revolt which began with Groen and Bakhuizen in the mid-nineteenth century has continued through later historians : Robert Fruin, G. W. Kernkamp, N. Japikse, H. Brugmans, the Calvinist historians A. A. van Schelven and J. C. H. de Pater, the Catholic historians W. F. J. Nuyens and L. J. Rogier, H. A. Enno van Gelder and of course – best-known in the English-speaking world – Pieter Geyl. Geyl's *Geschiedenis van de Nederlandsche Stam*, sections of which have been translated into English, has had the most powerful influence on general opinion about the nature, causation and course of the Revolt. On military affairs, reference may be made to the great survey of Netherlands military history by F. J. G. ten Raa and F. de Bas, *Het Staatse Leger* (6 vols, Breda, 1911), especially volume I.

Amongst Belgian historians who have contributed most to the debate, Henri Pirenne, L. P. Gachard, Kervyn de Lettenhove – *Les Huguenots et les Gueux* (6 vols, 1883–5) – and L. van der Essen must take first place amongst political historians. Dr J. A. van Houtte, like T. S. Jansma on the Dutch side, has done invaluable work in clarifying the economic and social aspects of the Revolt see, e.g., their contributions in the monumental *Algemene Geschiedenis der Nederlanden* (12 vols, 1949–58).

A detailed analysis in English of the historiography of the Revolt, including the work of the foregoing scholars, will be found in the valuable paper by Dr J. W. Smit in *Britain and the Netherlands*, ed. J. S. Bromley and E. H. Kossmann (1959). This volume and its later companion volume (1964), products of the conferences of Dutch and English historians which take place at intervals, contain indispensable material on Anglo-Netherlands relations. Equally valuable are two studies of cultural and political relations between England and the Netherlands published under the auspices of Professor A. G. H. Bachrach's Thomas Browne Institute at Leiden : J. A. van Dorsten's *Poets, Patrons and Professors* (1962) and *Leicester's Triumph* by J. A. van Dorsten and R. C. Strong (1964). Finally, among recent works on the *Revolt* between William's death and the Truce of 1609 Mr Jan den Tex's *Oldenbarneveldt* (vols I and II, Haarlem, 1960–2) must rank as a master work.

Central to any survey of English writing on the Revolt is *The Birth of the Dutch Republic* (Raleigh Lecture before the British Academy, 1946) by Sir George Clark, doyen of Anglo-Netherlands studies. It contains many penetrating insights and carries an excellent critical apparatus of bibliographical reference. Other studies in English with a direct bearing on the Netherlands are Dame Veronica Wedgwood's biography of William the Silent (1944) by the side of which can be placed the earlier biographies by Ruth Putnam (1895), P. J. Blok (1919–20 and F. Rachfahl (1906–14). Rachfahl's *Wilhem von Oranien und der Niederländische Aufstand* is not only a massive biography of the Prince but also a survey of the economic and social conditions of the Netherlands nobility which still has considerable value.

Amongst earlier English-speaking historians of the Revolt, none can compare with John Lothrop Motley. In spite of errors and anachronisms, Motley's works, especially in our connection *The United Netherlands* (4 vols, 1860–7), remain the most comprehensive and readable account in English. Quite apart from their literary quality, and regarded simply as an exercise in original scientific historical research, they remain a milestone in historiography. Another work from an earlier generation is C. R. Markham's *The Fighting Veres* (1888), an important contribution to the military aspects of the Revolt in spite of a misleadingly trivial title.

Representing as they did a major challenge to English diplomacy, Netherlands affairs have necessarily occupied the attention of our leading scholars of the Tudor period, not least in recent years. My pages therefore contain frequent reference to the work of such scholars as Sir John Neale, Professor J. B. Black, Dr A. L. Rowse, Dr Conyers Read, Garrett Mattingley, Professor R. B. Wernham and others. Professor Wernham's work in recent years as editor of the *Calendar of State Papers (Foreign)* has left all students of the subject in his debt. Although my opinions have differed from theirs on numerous points, I gladly pay tribute to their work, without which my own would have been impossible.

A number of relatively recent studies refer in one way or another to the relationship between the political, economic and social changes of the times, which are in turn closely related to English policy towards the Revolt. A full bibliography of these changes in the Netherlands will be found in the survey at the end of Dr J. A. van Houtte's *Economische en Sociale Geschiedenis van de Lage Landen* (Zeist and Antwerp, 1964). Particular attention may be drawn to the studies specified in this bibliography by E. Coornaert (on the New Draperies in the south Netherlands), C. Verlinden's *Crises économiques et sociales en Belgique à l'époque de Charles-Quint*, and the researches into sixteenth-century price movements by the same author in partnership with J. Craeybeckx and E. Scholliers (*Annales*, 1955). The most recent work on Antwerp is Dr H. van der Wee's *The Growth of the Antwerp Market and the European Economy* (3 vols, The Hague, 1963). A compendious account of Antwerp will be found in Professor S. T. Bindoff's chapter in vol II of the *New Cambridge Modern History* (1958). Attempts to explain political developments in the Netherlands in Marxist-materialist terms may be found in E. Kuttner's *Het Hongerjaar 1566* (Amsterdam, 1949) and T. Wittman's *Les Gueux dans les 'Bonnes Villes' de Flandre 1577–1584* (Budapest, 1969). O. de Smedt's *De Engelse Natie te Antwerpen* (2 vols, Antwerp, 1950) is useful for a survey of England's problems of commercial policy towards Spain and for an account of the different influential parties in the Netherlands' struggle. J. H. Kernkamp's *De Handel op de Vijand* (Utrecht, 1931) is the classic study of Dutch trade with Spain which proved a permanent irritant in Anglo-Dutch relations. A more recent study of the relationship between trade and war is that by F. Snapper, *Oorlogsinvloeden op de Overzeese Handel van Holland 1551–1719* (Amsterdam, 1959).

An extensive periodical literature in Dutch, Belgian, British, American and German learned journals (including some local and regional journals) touches on almost all aspects of the Revolt and is specified in detail in the notes to my text.

Index